PLOT TWIST

The Freedom You
Never Saw Coming

By

LINDSAY TAYLOR

PLOT TWIST
The Freedom You Never Saw Coming

To request permissions, contact the publisher at publish@joapublishing.com

Hardcover ISBN: 978-1-967575-58-9
Paperback ISBN: 978-1-967575-57-2
eBook ISBN: 978-1-967575-59-6

Printed in the USA.
Joan of Arc Publishing
Meridian, ID 83646

www.joapublishing.com

✦ Enjoy Exclusive Bonuses! ✦

Thank you for reading *Plot Twist.*
As a special thank you, I've created exclusive
bonuses just for you.

How to Access Your Book Bonuses

Simply scan the QR code below with your phone to
unlock your special resources:

TABLE OF CONTENTS

Dedication...ix

Prologue..xi

Chapter 1: The Disconnection That Broke Us..............................1

   The First Fracture..2

   The Age of Numb 2

   When the Soul Forgets...3

   When Religion Wounds..5

   God-Breathed..11

Chapter 2: When the Spirit Moves 15

Chapter 3: The Locked Up Life..22

Chapter 4: The Prison That Broke Me Open 30

   The Divine Setup 31

   The Breaking and Becoming 33

Chapter 5: The Heart of the Matter...41

   Freedom Truth 47

   Soul Fragmentation..48

Chapter 6: Where Freedom Begins.......................................55

Chapter 7: Testimonies That Tear Down Prison Walls...............62

Chapter 8: A Soul Set Free: Nate's Plot Twist...........................71

The Early Fracture 71

Rebellion in the Name of Freedom..............................72

The First Overdose: Salvation 73

The Second Overdose: Surrender 74

Into the Wilderness 74

Spiritual Warfare is Real..75

His Way Redemption Ranch...78

Chapter 9: Freedom in the Fight...79

The Belt of Truth 81

The Breastplate of Righteousness.................................83

The Shoes of Peace 84

The Shield of Faith 86

The Helmet of Salvation 87

The Sword of the Spirit..89

Chapter 10: Prison to Purpose: Jason Smith's Plot Twist 92

Chapter 11: Dope to Freedom: Jason Rudeen's Plot Twist........108

Chapter 12: Sidewalk Shackles to the Savior:
Corrine's Plot Twist 121

Chapter 13: The Truth That Couldn't Be Burned:
Karissa's Plot Twist..125

Chapter 14: The Real Wealth: Lindsay's Plot Twist...................137

Chapter 15: Healing Against All Odds: Brooke's Plot Twist..... 145

Chapter 16: The Key to the Lock 161

Surrender and Obedience 161

The Power of Surrender 163

A Step of Obedience: Baptism.. 164

Chapter 17: The Freedom Climb 173

The Freedom Toolbox 180

Mind & Heart Prisons... 182

Financial Prisons... 197

Relational Prisons 205

Behavioral Prisons 210

Situational Prisons 216

Spiritual Prisons.. 221

Freedom in Chains: Paul's Story 224

Closing Word... 227

Dedication

To my husband and children: the anchors of my heart and the light that keeps me rising.

To every soul who trusted me with your story—
Thank you for allowing me to share pieces of your heart and powerful testimonies.
You remind us all that even in our darkest prisons, hope still breathes.

And to those facing a prison,
whether behind literal bars or the invisible walls within,
know this: no one is beyond redemption.
God's love can reach you right where you are,
and freedom is possible, even here, even in the middle of the mess.

Prologue

Dear Fellow Freedom Seeker,

If you're holding this book, chances are your soul is longing for peace. Not the kind that comes from a quiet room or a good night's sleep—but the kind that settles deep within you. The kind that allows you to finally exhale after carrying too much for too long.

Maybe you feel trapped by something you can't quite name—or something you know all too well. Addiction. Grief. Shame. Fear. Debt. Exhaustion. Or the quiet ache of wondering if your heart will ever feel light again.

The walls may be visible or not, but you can feel them pressing in. You wake up with the same heaviness you carried to bed. Your thoughts pace like a prisoner in a cell, wearing a path in your mind. And somewhere deep inside, a whisper keeps asking, "Will it ever change".

I know what it's like to feel imprisoned without bars. I've lived seasons where grief pressed in so tightly I could barely breathe— losing my son four and a half years ago forever changed my life. Currently, I'm walking through financial rock bottom where the reality is crushing. In earlier chapters of my life, I lived in the mental prison of debilitating anxiety and fear.

Different seasons. Same feeling. Trapped.

This book isn't written from a mountaintop. It's written from the valley—while I'm still walking, still learning, still surrendering. Writing these pages became a plot twist of its own. I didn't realize how bound I was financially until the ground fell out beneath me, just as I began this book. These words met me in my own mess, and I hope they meet you in yours. We're in this together—as fellow travelers.

Throughout these pages, I'll speak openly about God and Jesus—not from a place of religion, but from lived relationship. I know that faith language can bring comfort for some and resistance for others. If you carry doubts or wounds from church or religion, I see you. You don't have to force belief or silence your questions here.

Take what resonates.

Leave what doesn't.

Trust that whatever is meant for you will meet you right where you are.

The apostle Paul once wrote from a literal prison that his chains did not define his freedom—his heart did. His circumstances didn't change, but something inside him did. That's the kind of freedom we're talking about here. Not escape. Not perfection. But peace that can exist even when life is still hard.

As you read, I invite you to go slowly. Pause when you need to. Set the book down if something stirs. You are not behind. You are not failing. Healing doesn't rush.

My prayer is simple: that somewhere in these pages, you feel seen. That your breath deepens. That hope flickers. And that you begin to discover a freedom you never saw coming—not because your circumstances changed, but because something inside you did.

You are not your worst moment.

You are not your deepest wound.

You are a sacred soul—worthy, loved, and not beyond redemption.

Let's walk this road together.

Prayer

Jesus,

Meet the reader right where they are.

Let Your presence be their safety, not pressure.

Turn their chains into a testimony—when the time is right.

Amen.

xiv

CHAPTER 1

The Disconnection That Broke Us

There was a time we remembered who we were. Before the masks. Before the shame. Before the prisons we built around our minds, our hearts, our homes, our nations. We were once connected—body, soul, and spirit. We were in alignment with the Divine. We walked with God, not just beside Him but within Him; intimately, honestly, whole. We knew who we were because we hadn't yet forgotten where we came from. But along the way, we became disconnected. And that disconnection broke us.

Due to this disconnection, we all face prisons:

- **Mind & heart:** self-hatred, shame, fear, perfectionism, hopelessness.

- **Finances:** debt, poverty, the belief our worth is tied to performance.

- **Relationships:** codependency, rejection wounds, toxic cycles.

- **Behavior:** addictions, avoidance, control, the numbing hum of survival mode.

- **Situations:** illness, abuse, homelessness, incarceration.

- **Spirit:** feeling abandoned by God, religious hurt, disconnection from truth.

THE FIRST FRACTURE

The first prison humanity ever entered wasn't one made of stone or steel. It was a separation. In the story of Eden, Adam and Eve didn't just disobey, they lost connection with God, with truth, and with the purity of their being. Shame entered the world, and they hid. Nakedness, once symbolic of freedom and vulnerability, became something to cover. To hide. To fear. That ancient rupture wasn't just theological. It was deeply human. And it has echoed through time ever since.

Whether you believe in the Garden or not, we've all lived that moment. That moment when something in us broke, when we stopped feeling safe in our own skin. When we forgot we were loved. When we began believing we had to earn our worth. When the Light became dim. That moment, both individually and collectively, was the beginning of our captivity.

THE AGE OF NUMB

Think about our world today. We walk in a world that runs on disconnection. We are disconnected from our bodies: ignoring hunger cues, suppressing emotion, pushing away past pain. We are disconnected from each other: scrolling, performing, comparing, avoiding eye contact, mistrusting kindness. This separation from self and others creates a numbing effect. Numbing us from the world and disconnecting us from truth, and ultimately, God. From Love itself.

This disconnection has produced a soul-level starvation. We hunger for something real. We ache for meaning, for belonging, for healing. But we've forgotten where to turn. So instead, we turn to coping mechanisms that only deepen the void: addiction, achievement, people-pleasing, perfectionism, violence, silence. We've built prisons to protect ourselves from pain, only to become trapped by the very walls we constructed.

And here's the thing about those prisons: freedom doesn't always mean the chains fall off immediately. Sometimes it's learning to breathe and live with them still on. The shift begins the moment we say yes to God, a consciousness and wisdom higher than our own. The moment we choose to stop running and start trusting. Freedom is a decision before it's a destination, and it starts with surrender. We don't always get to choose our circumstances, but we do get to choose how we show up in them.

WHEN THE SOUL FORGETS

We were made in God's image—our truest self—referred to as *Imago Dei*. Imago Dei is a Latin phrase that means "Image of God". It comes from the biblical idea in Genesis 1:27, which says:

"So God created mankind in his own image, in the image of God he created them; male and female he created them." **(Genesis 1:27, NIV)**

At its core, Imago Dei teaches that every human being is created with divine worth, dignity, and purpose, because we are made to reflect aspects of God's nature. What this means is, you are not here by mistake. You are not an accident. You carry the fingerprints of the divine. Your soul, your creativity, your capacity to love, reason, create, forgive, and feel deeply, all reflect God's image in you.

"For we are God's handiwork, created in Christ Jesus to do good works, which God prepared in advance for us to do." **(Ephesians 2:10, NIV)**

When we forget the One who made us, we forget who we are. This forgetfulness births fear. Fear breeds shame and shame births hiding. And hiding gives rise to all the forms of bondage we see today:

Addiction

Self-hate

Isolation

Shame

Depression

Division

Greed

Violence

None of these are the root problem. They are symptoms of a soul that has forgotten its Source. It is not a moral failing; it is a missing connection. And like any severed limb, the world is bleeding out because of what's been cut off.

WHEN RELIGION WOUNDS

It feels important to name one of the most painful disconnections of all: The one caused by *religion itself.* I have seen this disconnection time and again, especially the last four and a half years as I myself found my way back to God and eventually began to develop a relationship with Jesus.

What I've seen happen is those hurt by religion turn away from God altogether, when in reality, the damage was done by the people who claimed to represent Him. This may look like being shamed for having questions, dismissed for having doubts, told to sit down, be quiet, and fall in line. Maybe they were judged, not loved. Silenced, not seen. Taught fear instead of freedom. Control instead of compassion.

Some were told they were too broken to belong. Others were punished for being human. Many were taught that God's love had conditions and they would never quite measure up. When religion becomes more about rules than relationship, it stops reflecting the heart of God and starts building a prison instead.

I think of a friend I met on the island—the same island where I wrote much of this book—whose story stuck with me. He had been excommunicated from the Mormon church twice, and the pain of that loss ran deep. He wasn't angry at God initially; he loved his faith and wanted so desperately to do what was right. But over time, the striving broke him down. He was constantly trying to *earn* his way back into belonging, to prove himself worthy of love and acceptance.

In one of our conversations as we talked about faith and Jesus, he looked at me and said, "It's interesting because for so many Jesus is a source of Love and comfort but for me, **Jesus is my trauma."**

That struck me deeply. I felt the weight of what he was saying, and it made me reflect on the power spiritual leaders hold—and how the version of Jesus he was shown does not accurately represent who Jesus truly is. The rules. The expectations. The shame of never being enough. That does not reflect the true heart or character of Jesus. And I've heard this same ache echoed again and again—people who drifted from faith, not because Jesus ever spoke shame over them, but because those who claimed His name did. The wound felt like it was from Jesus, when in reality, it was from people and religious leaders representing Him.

I saw this truth again when I joined a group called Alpha—a safe, judgment-free space for anyone curious about faith to explore life's biggest questions: *Is there a God? Who is He? What does it mean to know Him?*

In that group, I met a couple who had grown up in the Mormon faith. The husband, much like my friend from the island, carried wounds from his experience. He believed he would never be "good enough" for God, and eventually reached a breaking point, thinking, *"If this is who God is—a God of judgment and unreachable standards—I don't want any part of it."*

But grace has a way of finding us when we least expect it. His wife found the church I now call home and we would end up meeting in our Alpha group. That decision changed everything. There, he encountered the true heart of God—not the version that had been misrepresented, but the One who meets us right where we are with love and compassion. Slowly, he started to rebuild a relationship with God, this time on a foundation of truth and grace, not rules and fear.

And it's not just one faith tradition where this happens. I've seen it across many—Christianity, Catholicism, Mormonism, and beyond. I want to pause here and say this clearly: both of the personal stories I've shared here (and Karissa's testimony in Chapter 9) come from individuals within the Mormon faith who experienced wounding through religion. At the same time, I have several friends in the Mormon faith who are deeply connected to God, richly filled by the Spirit, and genuinely nourished by their church community. What I'm sharing is not a reflection of the faith itself, but of how human systems—within any religion—can sometimes wound hearts when love gets replaced by control. In every denomination, there can be people who miss the heart of God's grace. When people are taught to earn what's already been freely given, love turns into labor and faith becomes exhausting. This isn't the way of Jesus.

It's worth repeating: Jesus didn't come to start a religion. He came to heal hearts. To tear down the walls that separate us from the love we were created for. He came to be in a relationship with people and restore connection: with God, with ourselves, and with one another. He came to free the oppressed, heal the wounded, and call the unseen by name.

If you've been hurt by church or religion, the truth is: **That was not God. That was people misusing His name.** The One who can set you free is not the same as the ones who hurt you. And while humans may have misrepresented Him, *Jesus still stands with open arms.* You don't have to have all the answers. You don't have to pretend. You don't have to walk back into a church building to find God. You can have doubts and questions. You just have to be willing to reconnect with Love itself. Because the truth is: God never left you.

As a child, I attended a Lutheran church with my family, but in my teenage years, I stepped away. I hadn't had a negative experience with church. I had a relationship with Jesus, but as I got older, I began to feel that God was much bigger than any one religion, including Christianity. I didn't believe in a single "right" way to connect with the Divine. Over time, I became more spiritual than religious, but in this pulling away, the disconnection happened. I didn't have a relationship with Jesus anymore and I went more than a decade without acknowledging God in my life. I never stopped believing, but the relationship was non-existent. In hindsight, I realize attending church helps keep me connected with truth, with peace, with freedom. And freedom has a name…Jesus.

Then, just before I walked into the darkest chapter of my life, God reached me in a profound way. By His grace, I found my way back—not to religion, but to a *relationship* with God. Even so, I carried resistance. I was hesitant to return to church, mainly because of this deep-seated belief that God is so much bigger than any one organization, along with a few other core teachings of Christianity that, as I write this book, I am still in process with.

Even stronger, I resisted Jesus because I equated Him solely with the structure of religion. But I've come to understand: a relationship with Jesus—the love, light, and restoration He brings—exists outside of any church. Jesus came to restore connection, reveal God's heart, and set captives free. His love has no borders. And yet, I deeply understand why people feel resistance toward God. Maybe it's because religion misrepresented Him. Maybe it's because you've found truth, compassion, or glimpses of the Divine in other places. If that's you, I honor that.

Here's what I've learned: You can walk through doubts, explore wisdom from different traditions, and still encounter His presence.

Jesus is the Way, the Truth, the Light (John 14:6 NIV). Not in an exclusive, weaponized sense, but in the truest sense, that His life, death, and resurrection reveal the deepest love we'll ever know. Personally, I have come to find that His words anchor me. His presence restores me. And His Spirit continues to transform me in ways nothing else ever has.

So while this book holds Jesus at the center, I want to reiterate that you don't have to have all the same language, beliefs, or answers to be here. My hope is that as you read, you'll feel the freedom to stay curious, to keep your heart open, and to allow God to meet you where you are. Because here's the truth: His love is bigger than our boxes. His grace reaches further than our doubts. And once you encounter Him, His Love fills you in ways nothing else ever could.

In time, I found my way back to church. A church that leads with love. A church that embraced me exactly as I was: doubts, imperfections, questions, and all. Their motto pierced my heart: *"No matter where you've been, what you've done, or what's been done to you, you belong here."*

But I'll be the first to tell you, I still wrestle with some of the core teachings. There are days when I question, doubt, or simply don't understand it all. For a long time, I thought that disqualified me. That I wasn't "Christian enough" to speak up, to serve, or to share the love of Jesus with others, especially in something as sacred as prison ministry.

I remember standing with my pastor, expressing my hesitation. "Who am I to go in and share about Christianity," I asked, "if I still struggle with parts of it?" He looked at me with such grace and said, "You're just in process. We all are." That moment shifted something in me. I realized I don't have to have it all figured out. None of us do.

God is so much bigger than what our human minds can grasp, and maybe we're not supposed to fully understand everything. Maybe faith is less about certainty and more about *trusting anyway*.

What I *do* know is this: A relationship with Jesus has radically transformed my life. His love, His grace, His redemption, His light; they've met me in the darkest corners of my story and pulled me into freedom. And I've watched Him do the same for countless others. That's what this book is about. Jesus didn't just come to save our souls and reconnect us with God, He came to bring heaven to us *now*, while we're still living, still struggling, still healing.

GOD-BREATHED

As I began writing *Plot Twist*, God started stirring things in my heart I wasn't expecting. I thought I was writing from a place of clarity, but the truth is, this book was written in the *middle* of my process. And because of that, it's God-breathed. Every page, every reflection, has stretched and grown me spiritually. Some of the very truths in these chapters are still working their way deeper into my own heart. It's been surprising, mind blowing and beautiful, all in one.

One day, in the middle of writing, I sat with a friend and shared the inner conflict I was feeling, torn between the beauty of my faith and the doubts of the beliefs I've carried for a long time in regard to religion. She said something I'll never forget, though I wish I could capture it all exactly the way she spoke it. The heart of her message was this:

"We're the ones who define religion as a box. We give it that meaning. But it doesn't have to be a box. The most important thing is YOUR relationship with God. That's yours. It's unique. It's sacred. Structure and boundaries can help, yes, but only if they're guiding you toward love, not fear. Keep your heart open. Keep seeking. Keep talking to God. He'll show you the way. It doesn't have to be complicated. Keep it simple."

That conversation freed something in me. I realized we each have our own relationship with God—it's not a collective checklist or a perfect performance. Yes, the Bible holds truth, and yes, there is deep wisdom in Scripture, but we tend to overcomplicate what was meant to be simple. At its core, faith is the willingness to surrender to a higher wisdom, to stay curious in the unknown, to keep showing up, and to let your heart stay open along the journey. And most importantly, it's learning to stay connected to Love itself—to receive it, become it, and extend it.

I've come to realize that many of my doubts weren't about God or even religion—they were rooted in the noise: the opinions and beliefs of others, layered with my own interpretations and questions. But when I began to open the Bible for *myself* and sit with God in prayer, without anyone else's lens shaping the experience, everything began to change. He started speaking directly to me—even powerfully answering my prayers. It has been nothing short of transformational. I've come to feel, deeply and sincerely, that I want to spend the rest of my life glorifying Jesus—letting Him work in me, and allowing that same love and light to flow out into the places where it's been lost.

Jesus saves. He restores. I've witnessed that truth over and over again, in my own life, and in the lives of so many others. So while Jesus is woven through every page of this book, this isn't a religious book.

It's a *human* book.

A *soul-help* book.

A *freedom* book.

If what I'm sharing in regard to the struggles and doubts around religion—or even the idea of having a relationship with Jesus—resonates with you, be sure to read chapter 12: *The Truth That Couldn't Be Burned.* It's an incredible chapter, featuring my friend Karissa's powerful testimony. She shares her journey of leaving the Mormon faith, along with her own surprise at discovering Jesus *still* at the very center of her spiritual journey after wanting nothing to do with Him for a long time.

Wherever you're coming from, whatever your background, beliefs, doubts, or wounds—you're welcome here. Truly. My hope is simple: that somewhere in these pages, in whatever way feels true to you, you catch a glimpse of something greater at work. Something that brings peace. That whispers hope. That gently calls your soul back home.

And finally, we must understand that our societal systems often reflect the state of our souls. Prisons, literal and metaphorical, are bursting at the seams. Mental health crises, broken families, mass incarceration, and generational trauma all trace back to this deep spiritual disconnection. Part of being human means we struggle, we stumble, and at times, we feel broken—but that brokenness is a "worldly" illusion. At the core, we are and have always been whole. The way out begins with reconnection to God and the true essence of who you are—already whole, already enough, already loved just as you are. That is the real plot twist.

CHAPTER 2

When the Spirit Moves

I continually sit in awe of God's presence and timing as I walk through life. Sometimes the Holy Spirit redirects us in ways we didn't plan. Not to withhold, but to protect, to guide, and to lead us into something greater than we could imagine. If we stay surrendered and listen, His leading will place us exactly where we need to be.

Paul experienced this in Acts 16:6–10:

Acts 16:6–7 (NIV)

Paul and his companions traveled throughout the region of Phrygia and Galatia, having been kept by the Holy Spirit from preaching the word in the province of Asia. When they came to the border of Mysia, they tried to enter Bithynia, but the Spirit of Jesus would not allow them to.

Acts 16:9 (NIV)

During the night Paul had a vision of a man of Macedonia standing and begging him, "Come over to Macedonia and help us."

Paul and his companions were told not to go preach the word of God in Asia, but in Macedonia instead. What looked like a closed door was actually a divine redirection toward the people God had prepared for them.

I've come to deeply understand that the Spirit's detours are never wasted; they're set-ups for encounters that align with God's heart and timing, something I experienced on my trip to Miami in preparation to write this book.

The birth of Plot Twist was part of a filming for a TV show called *Writers Island*. We stayed in Miami for a couple of days to pre-film before heading to the most sacred island in the British Virgin Islands to sit with God and begin writing. On our last evening in Miami, we decided to go to a Turkish spa for a cold plunge and sauna experience. What was meant to be a relaxing reset turned into a slightly sketchy adventure where we prayed not to leave with a mysterious disease. All jokes aside, it became a divine encounter that God used to communicate clearly the message I was supposed to bring through this book.

I had been praying every night, asking God to show me what my next book was meant to be. Ideas were flooding in, so many that I felt overwhelmed and unsure which direction to take. That morning in Miami, I prayed a little differently. I asked God to make it unmistakably clear. *No confusion, no guessing, just show me.*

That evening, as I sat in the sauna at the spa, a fellow author asked me the same question we'd all been tossing around that weekend:

"What are you going to write about?" I told her I wasn't entirely sure yet, that I was still waiting for the clarity, but I began sharing one of the messages that had been burning on my heart. As we spoke, a couple of guys walked in and sat nearby. We continued our conversation.

I was sharing about my passion for people who are incarcerated or living on the streets—those society often overlooks. I explained that one of my gifts is the ability to see people beneath their struggles. I don't judge where they've been, what they've done, or what their current circumstances are. I try to see them the way God sees them.

One of the men, perplexed, looked up at me and asked, "Can I ask what you guys are talking about?" I shared that we were headed to the British Virgin Islands to write books and film a documentary on the work we're doing. His friend jumped into the conversation and began sharing his story: he'd done time, had friends in gangs, and knows the grit of street life and survival. He's been in situations where he had to have a hardened heart to survive.

At first, he challenged and tested me. I shared that not only do I want to write a book for those incarcerated, but I am currently in the process of getting into prison ministry and want to speak to them personally. Like many people, he made assumptions based on my appearance, trying to make sense of what *"a woman like me"* was doing walking into prisons and doing this kind of work. I understood where he was coming from.

He told me flat out, "Those men don't care." He said they live in their heads, trapped in a constant storm of negativity, unable to show weakness, especially behind bars. Vulnerability could get them hurt. "These guys are tough," he said. "They always have to watch their backs." He was speaking to the harsh realities of prison life: the segregation, the survival mode, the gang mentality that runs deep in men's prisons. And he wasn't wrong.

I looked at him and said, "But what if they could be tough . . . and still know God? What if they could protect themselves and still walk with Jesus?"

As I said that, something shifted. He softened a bit.

And in that moment, he told me about an encounter he'd had with Jesus. He described how a powerful, overwhelming sensation had come over him. He explained how he had to step away because he was overcome with emotion as tears began to pour. He said it was a really moving and powerful moment for him. As he recalled the story, he paused mid-sentence.

"I'm getting chills right now just talking about it. Like a tingling all through my body."

I smiled and said, "That's the Holy Spirit."

He looked at me in awe, speechless for a moment, and then said, "You're like . . . an angel."

In that moment, I was overcome with emotion as I felt the Holy Spirit moving in that place. I knew this experience was the answer to the prayer I had poured out that morning, asking God for a clear sign.

To add to the magnitude of that moment, just that morning I had been having a conversation with a friend from JOA Publishing—similar to my friend in the sauna before the encounter with this gentleman—about what had been on my heart to write. Without knowing what would unfold later that day, she said, "Lindsay, you know what I'm hearing right now? You're like an angel sent to bring light to the forgotten."

And now, here I was, just hours later, face to face with a man who had lived the very life I was being called to speak into. The encounter led him to feel the truth and light in my words. I've come to understand deeply that we are simply the vessel—God works in and through us. When we listen and follow His call, He leads us exactly where we're meant to go.

We ended up talking for nearly an hour. He saw my heart. He heard the mission God has placed on my life. He was moved, and so was I. I walked away in awe of God and the power of the Holy Spirit, especially when we least expect it.

Jesus is after the heart. And when the heart opens, even in the heat of a sauna, the Spirit moves. It is through the open heart that transformation can begin. It's where the walls we build can fall, our pride softens, and truth is able to seep into the places pain once ruled. Jesus doesn't force His way in—He waits for the invitation. And when we finally open that door, even just a crack, His love floods in and begins to heal what we thought was unfixable. That night, I witnessed what happens when a hardened heart meets the tenderness of God's presence—how even in a moment that seemed ordinary, Heaven made itself known.

God reminded me that night that this **is what Jesus came for.** To love the hardened, the hurting, the forgotten, the angry. The ones behind bars, literal or invisible. Jesus didn't come to impress the religious or elevate the polished. He came to do heart surgery on all of us, because, let's be real, we all need it, and this includes those the world has given up on. And He'll do it anywhere: in a prison, a street corner, or a sauna.

This serves as a reminder that Divine appointments happen when we're surrendered and listening. We are not called to save people, we're called to see them. We as humans are the vessel here to work out into the world what Jesus has worked in and through us. The Spirit moves where hearts are open, not where circumstances are ideal. I have come to deeply know this truth: with an open heart, there is no place too dark for the Light of God.

I didn't go looking for that man. But God placed him in front of me as confirmation. Before I ever wrote a single word of this book, I had already encountered the mission. This book is about stepping into the darkest corners of our lives and illuminating the light.

Into the prisons.

Into the streets.

Into the hurting hearts.

You are *never* too far gone. The one who can bring total peace and freedom from anything is always at the door of your heart, waiting for you to open it up.

C H A P T E R   3

The Locked Up Life

After that deeply moving encounter with the man in the sauna, it stirred something deep in my spirit. I knew after that conversation that this was the book I was supposed to write, though I wasn't yet sure who exactly it was for. So I sat in stillness that night, heart wide open, and asked God, *"God, how do I write this book? Who am I writing to?"*

And I heard it clearly: *Write it to him.* Because in writing to him, I'm writing to all of us.

To the grieving.

To the incarcerated.

To the person trapped in financial fear.

To those shackled by addiction.

To the one drowning in self-hate.

To all buried under guilt.

To so many hiding behind suppressed emotions.

To every part of ourselves we've locked away because we deemed them unworthy of love.

We are all, at some level, prisoners.

Through both personal tragedy and professional experience as a social worker (which I will share more about in the next chapter), serving those facing addiction, homelessness, and mental health challenges, I've come to know this truth: No matter where we come from, no matter what we've done, we all began the same way. Created in the image of God, whole and deeply loved. We enter the world as innocent babies and toddlers, radiant with light.

Our human experience begins. Life happens. Trauma shapes us. Environments mold us. Some of us had the tools and support to break cycles. Others were born into the very cycles that broke us. But not one of us escapes this life unscathed. Not one of us goes through life without pain, without grief, without hardship. I call this our shared humanity.

And yet, beneath all the wounds, beyond the mistakes, deeper than the pain, we are souls longing for home. Longing to remember who we are. Longing to reconnect with our wholeness. On a spirit (or being) level, we are already whole. But the moment we develop conscious awareness—our sense of self, memory, and the ability to reflect on our thoughts (somewhere between eighteen months and three years old)—we begin to forget. We begin to drift from our true identity. We lose touch with our being.

We take on false identities:

"Not enough."

"Broken."

"Unworthy."

These are the illusions of the human experience and lies of the enemy which we will explore deeper in later chapters. They feel real, but they are not truth.

The truth is this: No matter what you've done, no matter what prison you're in, you are capable of change. Of healing. Of freedom. But here's the thing about freedom: It must be chosen. It usually doesn't show up as an open door. It comes during or after hard-fought battles that push you to your knees, sometimes shifting us into a place of surrender—which is actually a beautiful place to be, because it is in surrender that we allow Christ to lead the way. We quit relying on "self-help" and move into spirit-led healing.

There's a scripture I love that speaks directly to this kind of surrender: *"Trust in the Lord with all your heart, and lean not on your own understanding; in all your ways submit to Him, and He will make your paths straight."* – (Proverbs 3:5–6, NIV)

This verse reminds us that freedom doesn't come from figuring it all out. It doesn't come from solving every problem or changing every external condition. It comes from letting go of what we think we know and choosing to trust in the One who can see what we can't see. It's in handing over control that we begin to walk in alignment with God, with truth, with peace, and with purpose.

Life is like the game Operation. We try to remove the broken pieces without setting off alarms. We try not to mess up. But inevitably, we do. And when we do, the lie creeps in: "You're not enough." So we tuck those parts of ourselves away, into emotional solitary confinement. And those parts? They grow quiet. But not healed, just hidden.

And here's the truth: The vices we run to—alcohol, control, overworking, rage, image, suppression—aren't the root problem. They are bandages. The temporary comfort. The doors we walked through hoping to feel whole. But those doors didn't free us. They chained us deeper. Because what we thought would soothe us, splintered us.

And yet we stayed, because when we're stuck in our body and disconnected from our spirit, pain is familiar. And survival mode teaches us the cage is safer than the unknown. But here's the truth: you cannot heal what you refuse to see. You cannot free what you won't face. Freedom demands exposure. Light. Compassion. Not to fix the wounded parts, but to love them back to life.

We don't become prisoners because we're evil. We become prisoners because we forgot we are loved. And in forgetting our worth, we made silent agreements with our pain:

"Stay hidden, and I'll keep you safe."

"Stay quiet, and I'll keep you fed."

"Stay small, and I'll keep you loved."

That man in the sauna told me, "Prison is just a business." He meant the system. But I saw the metaphor. Inside of us, we're running businesses, too. Spiritual empires of suppression and survival, where we are both prisoner and warden, locked in self-made cells. But that is not where the story ends.

I once heard a phrase from my pastor, Pastor Chad Moore at Sun Valley Community Church, who I will reference at several points throughout these pages, that undid me. He said, "The message of the Bible is not shame on you. It's shame off you, in Jesus' name."

That resonated deeply. We often believe freedom means fixing everything on the "outside". But the real prison isn't out there, it's the guilt we carry in silence. The debt we owe. The secrets we've buried. The nights we can't forget. Guilt says, "I owe you." And over time, that debt builds like a wall, shutting the door to love and locking you inside your own shame.

But Jesus came to cancel that debt. To break that lock. To speak shame off of you. Pastor Chad's sermon titled, "How to Forgive Yourself", outlines how we can begin to walk out of bondage and into freedom:

1. **Identify the Debt.**

   What are you carrying? A secret? A regret? A betrayal? Name it; not to condemn yourself, but to release it.

2. **Face the Truth.**

   Jesus said, "Then you will know the truth, and the truth will set you free" (John 8:32). But first, it might make you uncomfortable. Because truth requires responsibility. But you are not being punished, you are being set free when you take responsibility and ask God to redeem you through facing that truth.

3. **Confess to God.**

    Psalm 32:5 says, *"Finally, I confessed all my sins to You... and You forgave me! All my guilt is gone."* Jesus isn't waiting to rub your nose in the past, He's waiting to redeem it. And redemption goes beyond confessing to God and bringing your sin into the light; we must open our hearts so God can work in you and through you, changing and transforming you from the inside out. That's redemption.

4. **Confess to Someone You Trust.**

    There is healing in being seen. There is power in saying it out loud. Because what's hidden in darkness can only be healed in light.

Here's what I want you to know: The prison door you've been waiting for someone else to unlock? It was never locked from the outside. Jesus already broke the lock. He already paid the price. He already called you free. The only question left is: Will you walk out?

This is your plot twist. This is your moment. Not to perform your way out, but to surrender your way through.

Prayer of Release into Freedom

Jesus,

I come to You just as I am. No more hiding. No more pretending.

You know what I've done. You know what I carry. And still you call me loved.

Still, you choose me.

Today, I name the guilt that has weighed me down.

I bring to You the debt I've tried to carry on my own.

The things I've done. The words I've spoken. The pain I've caused, and the pain I've lived with in silence.

Forgive me, Lord.

I surrender it all to You.

Every lie I believed that said I was unworthy.

Every secret I thought disqualified me.

Every moment I replayed, thinking I was too far gone.

You already paid the price.

You already made the way.

So right now, I lay it down:

The guilt. The shame. The debt. The fear.

I give it to You, Jesus, the One who can set me free.

Wrap me in Your mercy.

Cover me in Your grace.

Remind me that I am not what I've done,

I am who You say I am: Redeemed. Forgiven. Free.

Help me walk in truth.

Help me tell someone I trust.

Help me live like someone who's been released from prison;

because I have.

Thank You, Jesus,

for loving me too much to leave me chained.

I choose freedom.

I choose You.

Amen.

CHAPTER 4

The Prison
That Broke Me Open

The truths in chapter 3 aren't just theology to me. They've been lived, tested, and wrestled out in real time—in hospital rooms, in foster homes, on street corners, inside therapy offices, and in the deepest valleys of my own life.

Before we go any further, I want to step out from behind the framework for a moment and let you see more of my story. Because the prisons and the freedom I'm writing about here are not abstract concepts; they're the very ground that I, like many of you have walked on. I shared this part of my journey in my first book, *The Rise of a Soul Soldier*, but for those who haven't read it, I felt it was important to include it here as well.

Through the social work profession, I've walked with birth parents placing their children for adoption, teens battling suicidal ideation, and families navigating unspeakable pain. I've fostered a child, supported her parents through recovery, and witnessed reunification through grace and healing. I've sat with gang-involved teens and adults who were really just people looking for *love.* I've worked with those experiencing homelessness, incarceration, addiction, and profound grief. And through it all, one truth has echoed again and again: Beneath all our pain, we are souls longing to feel *love* and be *whole* again.

What I didn't realize was that God was preparing me through every one of those encounters. The lessons I had learned while walking others through their pain would soon become the compass guiding me through my own.

THE DIVINE SETUP

Just weeks before my life would forever change, God began stirring something in me I couldn't yet explain. It started in the most ordinary place—the gym—when my coach, who had never once talked about faith, suddenly brought up the Alpha group he was attending and rather adamantly encouraged me to join. He described it as a place where people could ask hard questions about life and faith, and I eventually felt the unexpected nudge to go. That simple "yes" opened a door I didn't even realize I needed—a slow turning of my heart back toward God, just before my world would be shattered.

A week later, God reached me through another unexpected avenue. One of my interns shared about visiting with a psychic medium who helped her process her grief of losing a friend. She began to encourage me to see him regarding a friend I had lost to suicide in 2018. I wasn't sure how I felt about seeing a psychic medium, but as she spoke and I listened, I felt that same deep inner tug—the kind that doesn't let go until you follow it. Against my usual reasoning, I booked an appointment.

When the session came, the medium knew nothing about me—just my first name. Yet what he said left me speechless. He mentioned the loses I had faced, pointed to my future work in suicide treatment, and then said something that didn't make sense at the time but would later change everything:

"They keep showing me a rainbow. There's something really strong with a rainbow. Pay attention to that."

I didn't understand it then, but I soon would. On May 2, 2021, I lost a student to suicide—a young soul I had poured into, cared for deeply, and believed in. The grief was crushing. I was already carrying the heaviness of that loss when, just one week later, the unthinkable happened. I found myself standing in the ICU beside my own son, praying for a miracle.

And that's when it happened. In the early hours of Mother's Day morning May 9, 2021, waiting to get back into our son's ICU room, exhausted and heartbroken, my husband suddenly said in disbelief, "Look up at the window." I lifted my eyes, and across the glass in big letters were the words: **#lookfortherainbow.**

At that moment, everything stood still. A brief sense of peace washed over me. The message was too precise, too personal to be coincidence. That was the first time I felt God's presence break through the devastation—meeting me in the darkest night of my life with a sign of hope that would carry me through the years ahead.

From that day forward, the rainbow became sacred—a divine language between heaven and my heart. It would appear again and again at the most impossible, holy moments, reminding me that love never dies, that God is still near, and that even in unbearable grief, light will always find its way through. It was the defining moment for me that there is something far beyond our human comprehension to all our lives and stories.

THE BREAKING AND BECOMING

We would tragically lose our son Alex later that day at the young age of 17, to fentanyl poisoning.

Alex was a sweet soul—vibrant, witty, and full of life. His smile could disarm even the hardest day, and his laugh carried a joy that filled every corner of the room. He was a gifted gymnast—disciplined, determined, and received many medals that only hinted at the dedication behind them. But behind his radiant spirit lived a quiet ache, one that began long before drugs ever entered the picture.

From early childhood, Alex carried the wound of his biological mother's absence. I stepped into his life when he was just a toddler and loved him as my own, but the ache of that missing connection stayed with him as he grew. No matter how much love surrounded him, a part of him always felt a missing piece. That missing piece became the undercurrent of his life—an ache beneath the surface of his smile.

When Alex walked away from gymnastics, he lost more than a sport. He lost the identity that had once anchored him, the thing that made him feel strong, capable, and proud. Without that sense of purpose, he began to drift. Then came 2020. The world shut down, schools closed, and the isolation of the pandemic hit hard. Like so many teens, he was cut off from community, structure, and the everyday rhythm that keeps young people grounded. He began to get heavy into marijuana.

It started to take from him—the spark in his eyes, his laughter, his motivation. Over time, his personality began to shift. The joy that once defined him was replaced by agitation, confusion, and waves of despair. He began experiencing marijuana-induced psychosis and deep mental health struggles. We watched our boy turn into someone we barely recognized. Looking back, I often say that while fentanyl ultimately took his life, the marijuana caused a great deal of destruction and took him from us first.

By early 2021, Alex was fighting an invisible war. He wanted to be okay. He wanted peace. But he didn't yet have the tools to face the storm inside him. In March, he told my husband that he had tried fentanyl. He said it honestly—but with defeat—as though he already knew how dangerous it was and that it could kill him.

Just weeks later, our greatest fear became our reality. We received the devastating phone call that Alex had been brought to the hospital without a pulse. The medical team revived him after sixteen minutes, but there was no brain activity. For sixteen long hours, we stood by his side, watching the machines breathe for him. And then, we came face to face with the most heartbreaking decision of our lives: to unhook the machine.

As we prepared to say goodbye, I looked over at my husband standing on the left side of the bed, then down at Alex lying between us, and finally at myself on the right. The weight of the moment hit me: here we were on Mother's Day—a day that symbolized everything Alex longed for most in life, his mother—and once again, it was just Matt and me by his side, as it had been for the majority of his life. It broke my heart that Alex left this world on Mother's Day— a day that painfully mirrored his lifelong struggles.

I want to take a moment to honor her. Over the years, I've come to hold Alex's mom in my heart with deep love. She did the best she could in the capacity she was able, and her heart was broken, too. Her pain deserves acknowledgment in this story of heartbreak. We are all doing the best we can with the circumstances and struggles we face, and she is no exception.

Throughout his life, Alex and I shared a special bond. But I could never fill the void left by the longing for his mom—nor did I ever try to. I was his bonus mom. I raised him the best way I knew how, stepping into that role at just eighteen years old. I did my growing up right alongside him. There were seasons of deep closeness and seasons of tension, but through it all, I loved him fiercely. Over time, I came to realize that Alex was one of my greatest teachers. Raising him held up a mirror and invited me into my own healing.

In his final year, Alex carried anger and resentment toward me—some of it justified, some of it misplaced. That has been one of my heaviest griefs: the lack of closure, the things left unsaid. Grieving him meant grieving the unfinished pieces of our story too.

When my husband and I got married, we included a rose ceremony in our vows. Matt and I exchanged white roses—symbols of our promise to stand together through everything. I gave the boys yellow roses, representing my vow to love them unconditionally as their bonus mom till what I thought would be the end of my life. At 4:45 p.m. on May 9, 2021, as Alex's heart came to a stop, I stood by his side, something I had vowed and hoped to do until the end of my life, as surely he was supposed to outlive me. With immense love in my heart that spilled over as tears streamed down my face, I held his hand tightly.

That moment—standing by Alex's side, holding his hand as his heart stopped—is something I will hold very close to my heart for the rest of my life. It was a deeply heartbreaking experience, yet one filled with immense love. This tragic path has taught me that grief is love. As the saying goes, *"Where there is deep grief, there was great love."*

Although Alex's physical presence is gone, his spirit is woven deeply into the fabric of my life. His love, his lessons, and even the pain of losing him have become central to my life's work. Through losing a child, I've discovered a strength I never knew I had—a strength that allows me to hold my own grief while walking alongside the grief of others, guided by the light of Alex's love as my compass in both life and the work I do. He and God's presence, often through rainbows, continue to remind me that even in the deepest sorrow, love remains eternal.

There is life before Alex passed away, and life after. I will never be the same. That week didn't just break me—it stripped me to the bone, rearranged my entire world, and forever changed how I see— and move through—life. When you lose what you love most, you collapse. But if you allow God to meet you in that collapse, He begins to rebuild you—layer by layer—into something altogether new.

Through Alex's loss, my calling became even more clear: to bring love and light into the darkest corners of the world and the human heart. To reach those standing on the same edge my son once stood on and to remind them that they are not too far gone. His story became my mission. His absence became my awakening.

Recently, I stepped away from my role as Clinical Director of a suicide treatment center to fully follow that calling. I founded the Soul Soldier Network and wrote my first book, *The Rise of a Soul Soldier,* to help others rise from the ruins.

This book continues that mission—because I know how dark life can get. And I know the One who pierces the darkness every single time. The One who saves. The One who restores. The One who sets us free.

In the aftermath of everything that broke me open, I began to understand freedom differently. It wasn't something I would feel my way into. It was something I would have to stand my way into.

Paul's words in Philippians Chapter 4 began to take on new meaning for me—especially knowing he wrote them from prison:

> "Therefore, my brothers and sisters, you whom I love and long for, my joy and crown, stand firm in the Lord in this way, dear friends." (Philippians 4:1)

Paul doesn't tell us to stand firm in our strength, our understanding, or our ability to cope. He tells us to stand firm in the Lord. Freedom, I learned, isn't passive. It's guarded. Standing firm meant choosing not to retreat when grief, fear, or old patterns tried to pull me back into captivity. Some days, standing firm looked like nothing more than staying rooted in truth when everything inside me felt unstable.

Grief didn't remove joy—but it redefined it. Paul goes on to say:

> *"Rejoice in the Lord always. I will say it again: Rejoice!"*
> (Philippians 4:4)

This isn't denial. Paul is imprisoned. Rejoicing isn't about pretending circumstances are okay; it's about anchoring joy to its true source. I learned that joy is not a mood—it's a spiritual posture. I could grieve deeply and still rejoice defiantly—not because life made sense, but because God, the author of redemption, was still at work. Joy no longer depended on what I had lost, but on the One who sustains me.

That tension between grief and joy became real to me through the lyrics of the song *"21 Years"* by TobyMac. He wrote the song after losing his son to fentanyl. The lyrics say:

21 years makes a man full grown.

21 years, what a beautiful loan.

21 years, I loved every one.

Thank you, Lord, for my beautiful son.

As those words played through my heart, I felt something rise in me that surprised me—not sorrow alone, but deep gratitude. We are loaned this life and everything in it—including our children. Every time I hear those lyrics, they echo both the ache and the deep gratitude I carry for Alex:

17 years makes a boy full grown.

17 years, what a beautiful loan.

17 years, I loved every one.

Thank you, Lord, for my beautiful son.

It's incredible what happens when we turn our eyes to what's eternal—when we shift our perspective from what we've lost to what we were given, from what we didn't get to the miracle of what we did. Gratitude doesn't erase grief, but it does transform it. This, I've learned, is what it means to rejoice in the Lord—not by denying pain, but by anchoring joy in Him, the eternal home of our souls.

As the days turned into months, I also had to relearn what strength actually meant. This Scripture became one of the most honest invitations I've ever encountered:

> *"I know what it is to be in need, and I know what it is to have plenty. I have learned the secret of being content in any and every situation... I can do all this through Him who gives me strength."* (Philippians 4:12–13)

Paul isn't talking about achievement here. He's talking about endurance. Contentment isn't complacency—it's dependency. Strength isn't self-sufficiency; it's Christ-sufficiency. I didn't have to change or escape my situation to be sustained in it. I didn't have to have answers to be held. His strength met me precisely where mine ran out.

This chapter is not just the story of what shattered my life. It is the story of how freedom began to take root—not by removing the pain, but by teaching me how to stand, how to rejoice without denying grief, and how to depend on a strength beyond my own.

Losing Alex didn't just break my heart—it broke everything open. His story became the turning point that forced me to see not just the prisons we live in, but the deeper battles happening inside the human heart. If I was going to heal, if I was going to help others heal, I had to go deeper than the grief, deeper than the circumstances, and into the place where everything begins: the heart.

CHAPTER 5

The Heart of the Matter

The plot twist always begins in the place you least expect: your own heart. This truth stirred in me after hearing a sermon by Pastor Chad Moore, titled: "What's Really Causing the Chaos in Your Life", which inspired this chapter.

If you've ever wondered why you think the way you do . . . why you speak the way you do . . . why you keep repeating the same patterns that you swore you were done with, it all goes back to one place: the heart. Not the one pumping blood through your chest, but the one buried deep inside your soul. The place where your wounds live. The place where truth and lies wrestle. The place where freedom begins or where bondage stays hidden.

Scripture puts it like this: "Above all else, guard your heart, for everything you do flows from it" (Proverbs 4:23). Everything. Your habits. Your reactions. Your relationships. Your triggers. Even your addictions.

Behavior change without heart change is exhausting. Real transformation happens when God has full access to the root of our hearts. Guarding your heart isn't just about protecting yourself from harm, it's about preserving the sacred place where your spirit, soul, and body align under God's design.

In God's original blueprint, the spirit was meant to lead, the soul to agree with truth, and the body to follow in peace—something we will explore deeper in the next chapter. But when sin entered the story, that order was reversed, and the heart became the battleground. This is why Scripture calls us to guard it "above all else", because what flows from it touches every part of who we are.

Remember as discussed in chapter 1, that your worth is anchored in the One who made you. This is the heart of every Plot Twist—not just getting out of a prison, but remembering you were never made for one. The enemy works hard to get you to forget this, because if he can steal your identity, he can keep you locked in cycles of shame, striving, and self-sabotage. Guarding your heart is guarding your identity. It's choosing to filter what comes in so that what flows out reflects the truth of who you already are in Him. This is something we will explore deeper in chapter 8.

As the Psalmist prayed: "Create in me a pure heart, O God, and renew a steadfast spirit within me" (Psalm 51:10, NIV). That's not just a request for God to make us better, it's an invitation for Him to realign us to His original design, where the Spirit leads, the soul agrees with His truth, and the body walks it out in freedom.

Have you ever replayed a hurtful conversation over and over in your mind like a broken record you can't stop? Ever caught yourself snapping in anger, then wondering where it even came from? Ever sabotaged something good, not because you didn't want it, but because deep down you didn't believe you deserved it?

That's your heart talking.

That's pain leaking out.

That's the proof that something inside needs healing.

We live in a culture obsessed with surface-level fixes. Pastor Chad pointed out that religion can sometimes teach us how to behave better, how to clean up the outside, and how to keep it all together. But Jesus? He's not in the business of behavior modification. He's after transformation. Real, soul-deep, heart-level transformation. Because Jesus knows the truth: your behavior is just fruit. Your heart is the root. And unless you let Him dig into the root, the fruit will keep showing up, rotten and bitter.

As Pastor Chad noted— Anger, envy, guilt, greed, jealousy, and shame all live deep in the heart. And the enemy loves to keep them there, whispering lies that justify our pain and block our healing. He goes on to point out that heart disease is deadly even when you feel fine. You can look healthy. Function well. Even smile through it. But inside, something's blocked. Something's slowly breaking you down. And without intervention, it will destroy you.

One of the most dangerous blockages of the heart is unforgiveness. Jesus addresses this directly in Matthew 18 when Peter asks, *"Lord, how many times shall I forgive my brother or sister who sins against me? Up to seven times?"* Peter thinks he's being generous. In Jewish tradition, three times was sufficient. Peter doubles it and adds one. Seven. Jesus replies, *"I tell you, not seven times, but seventy-seven times."* With that single statement, Jesus dismantles the ledger.

In Genesis, vengeance was multiplied "seventy-seven times." Jesus flips the script. Where the world multiplies retaliation, the kingdom multiplies mercy. Forgiveness in His kingdom is not arithmetic. It is identity.

Because when we count offenses, we are still holding onto control. We replay the wound. We rehearse the injustice. We keep a quiet record. It feels like strength. It feels like protection. But internally, something tightens. Unforgiveness constricts the heart long before it shows up in behavior.

Jesus then tells a story about a servant whose impossible debt—ten thousand talents—is completely canceled. It was an absurd amount. Lifetimes of income. The servant doesn't ask for cancellation; he asks for time. But the master gives mercy instead and absorbs the loss himself.

That's grace.

But then the same servant grabs another man who owes him a fraction and begins to choke him, demanding repayment. The debt was real. The wound was real. But compared to what had just been forgiven, it was small. The tragedy wasn't the second debt. It was that mercy received never transformed the first servant's heart. When grace doesn't penetrate, it calcifies.

The parable ends with imprisonment. And that is not accidental. Because spiritually, that's what bitterness does. You relive the offense. You rehearse the moment. You replay the hurt. Meanwhile, the other person may be living freely, but your heart remains chained.

Forgiveness is not pretending it didn't hurt. It is refusing to let it own you. It does not eliminate boundaries. It eliminates bitterness. It does not excuse injustice. It surrenders justice to God.

Jesus ends with this piercing truth: forgive from the heart.

In Hebrew understanding, the heart is the center of will, emotion, and identity. Heart-level forgiveness means you stop weaponizing the memory later. You stop secretly wishing harm. You stop rehearsing superiority. It doesn't erase what happened. It releases vengeance.

And this is where love becomes central to our healing. Because sometimes the prisons we live in weren't built from what we did. They were built from what was done to us. And while you were never responsible for the wound, you are responsible for what you do with it now.

The more aware you are of your canceled debt, the less interested you become in collecting someone else's. The more deeply you understand that you were rescued—not self-repaired—the softer your heart becomes. Forgiveness doesn't minimize pain. It maximizes freedom. And love is the only force strong enough to unlock that cell.

That's why Jesus came. Not to put a bandage on your pain. Not to teach you how to pretend. But to perform spiritual heart surgery. To help you connect back with your wholeness in and through Him.

And this is where love becomes central to our healing. While writing this book, a striking truth came through: the prisons we find ourselves trapped in often trace back to a single root—a hunger for love. Beneath layers of anger, shame, addiction, or fear is usually an unmet longing to be seen, valued, and loved. Love is perhaps the deepest desire of the human heart, an ache woven into our very design.

And as long as we keep part of us locked away, the lies keep us bound. But here's the hope: true healing comes when love, God's love, touches those very places. When His light shines into the cell we've created inside ourselves. Because no matter what darkness you've locked away, the light is always there, waiting to break in. Love is the greatest commandment in all of Scripture. It is the foundation, the filter, and the fruit of true faith. Anything that produces shame, fear, or condemnation misses the heart of Jesus—because His way has always been love.

Jesus rewires our whole system. He goes to the root, not the surface. He doesn't condemn the part of you that fell short; He rescues it, redeems it, and stitches it back together with love. Because here's the truth: you are whole. You always have been, and you always will be.

Love isn't just a feeling. It's the oxygen of freedom. Without it, we keep gasping for air in all the wrong places. With it, we finally breathe. With it, we finally live.

FREEDOM TRUTH

Most of our prisons are built on three foundations: lack of self-worth, misdirected love, and the lies we've believed about ourselves.

Lack of self-worth is one of the most subtle yet powerful traps of the human heart. When we forget who we are in God, we begin searching for worth in everything else—success, approval, performance, relationships, appearance, even spirituality. We chase validation, thinking it will fill the ache, but it never lasts. The truth is, when you don't know your worth, you'll settle for chains that feel familiar instead of freedom that feels uncertain. This is exactly what the enemy wants—to convince you that you're not enough, so you'll keep hustling for love you already have. Healing begins the moment you remember that your value was set by the One who created you, and no mistake, failure, or label can change that.

Misdirected love is what happens when the heart's deepest longing—to be known and loved—is pointed toward things that can never truly satisfy. We give our devotion to people, possessions, passions, or purposes that were never meant to carry the weight of our souls. It's not that love itself is wrong—it's that we've misplaced it. We've tried to make temporary things fill an eternal need. When love is directed away from its true Source, it binds instead of frees. But when love is redirected back to God—the Author of love itself—it becomes healing, purifying, and liberating. His love doesn't demand that you earn it; it reminds you that love is your essence—you are love.

The lies we've believed happened when we took on false identities—"I'm unworthy," "I'm too broken," "I'll never be enough"—and began living from those illusions instead of from truth. These lies became the scripts that shaped our choices, our relationships, and the way we see ourselves. But lies lose their power the moment they're brought into the light. When truth enters, illusion shatters. God's Word reminds us that we are fearfully and wonderfully made, chosen, and redeemed. The journey of freedom begins when we stop agreeing with the lies and start aligning with the truth of who we've always been in Him.

Freedom Prayer

Jesus, I invite You into the deepest places of my heart.

Touch the parts I've hidden away in shame, the parts I thought disqualified me from love.

Heal the wounds that lack of self-worth carved into me.

Break the chains of every false place I've searched for love,

and anchor me in Your love that sets me free.

Today, I choose to let Your love unlock my prison.

SOUL FRAGMENTATION

The next problem we bump up against is getting caught up in our soul, specifically our mind. We want the strategy, the steps, the roadmap. We long to understand what comes first, what comes next, what comes last. We want to think our way through the pain . . . the confusion . . . the addiction . . . the loss.

A guarded heart keeps us from growth, thus the only way forward is vulnerability. Not performance. Not perfection. Not pretending. But soul-baring, truth-telling, messy, beautiful honesty. Vulnerability is what cracks the armor we've built to survive. It's the courage to be seen without a filter—to stop managing our image and start revealing our humanity. It's the surgical tool. The breakthrough. Where we make space for God to meet us and do what only He can do. You can't access freedom through logic, you access it through feeling and honesty. You access it when you say, "I'm not okay," and let someone see you there. You access it when you cry out to God in the dark and realize He was never gone. You access it when you share the stories you swore you'd never tell: the shame, the loss, the grief, the love you never received. When you open, others open. When you tell the truth, others find theirs.

That's why stories of truth and vulnerability will be shared throughout these pages, because through others' stories of imprisonment and pain, you will see that freedom from ANYTHING you are facing in life is possible. Freedom is never about pretending you're fine. It's about being real and being met there by a God who already knows. And here's what I've seen over and over again, in my own story and in the lives of others: every time someone breaks free from their personal prison, God is often at the center of their story.

Jesus is standing at the door of your heart, asking to come in and cleanse what's been festering. To heal what's been hurting. To love what's felt unlovable. And to begin a transformation that starts right here . . . with heart work. So, if you're willing—this is where we begin. Not with behavior modification. Not with appearance. But with the part of you that hurts most and hopes most: your heart. This is soul work. The excavation. The opening. And ultimately, the freedom you were created for.

So I would encourage you to open your hands and ask: "What is the better way?" Then listen. Let's go there, together. And as you move forward, remember: this is not about fixing yourself, it's about reconnecting with the YOU who is *already loved, whole and free*. The heart work is holy work. It's where heaven meets humanity, and where the story starts to turn. This is where your plot twist begins.

The Anchor Prayer

A simple practice to help you connect with God and find peace.

Before moving forward, I want to offer you a gentle way to begin or end your day—or return to whenever you feel overwhelmed or your emotions start to take over—so you can anchor yourself in truth, peace, and spiritual connection.

Take a moment now to settle your heart.

Close your eyes if it feels comfortable.

Begin with a slow, deep breath in—

breathing in God's presence.

Allow His presence to fill your body, from the soles of your feet to the top of your head

Simply receive.

Now slowly breathe out—

releasing anything that is not of God (fear, doubt, confusion).

Let go of whatever is no longer serving you.

Surrender what you don't need to carry.

Hold for just a moment.

Now take a second deep breath in—

breathing in God's peace.

Draw that peace all the way in,

allowing it to soften every place of worry, fear, doubt, and tension.

Let peace settle where your body has been holding stress.

And as you breathe out—

release fear, doubt, anxiety, and heaviness.

Let it flow out of your body, all the way through the soles of your feet.

Imagine it leaving completely, making space for calm.

Now take one more slow, intentional breath in—

breathing in God's love and light.

Allow that light to radiate through your body,

filling the spaces that need love,

touching the places that feel tired, guarded, or heavy.

And as you breathe out—

release anything that still needs to go.

Invite God's light to shine through every place of resistance, pain, or

holding.

Let His light gently carry away what no longer belongs.

Now, gently place your hands open on your lap, palms facing

upward—a simple posture of receiving.

Let your shoulders soften.

Allow your body to rest.

Now softly say:

Come, Holy Spirit.

Meet me right here.

Help me see what I need to see.

Help me hear what I need to hear.

Guide me into truth.

Then sit in stillness for a moment.

You don't have to force anything.

Just breathe.

Trust that even silence speaks.

God already knows what your heart needs.

His presence doesn't rush.

He meets you in the quiet.

Stay here for a few moments.

If something comes to mind—a word, a feeling, an image, or even a sense of peace—receive it gently. There's no pressure to "get it right." Simply notice.

When you're ready, open your eyes slowly.

Take a moment to write down anything that surfaced.

Then open your Bible or a Bible app and ask:

God, show me what You want me to know today through your word.

Don't overthink it.

Let your intuition guide you.

Turn to the first page that opens, or scroll through the books in your app and pause where something catches your attention.

Trust what stands out, and allow yourself to land exactly where you're meant to be.

And if understanding Scripture feels hard (you're not alone), take the verse or passage you were led to and invite support. You can ask Google or ChatGPT to help break it down by requesting:

- Context around the verse

- Life application

- Two or three journal reflections

This is how we return to God's presence.

This is how we learn to listen.

This is how we begin anchoring our lives in truth.

Come back to this practice whenever your soul feels scattered, heavy, or tired.

Let it be your meeting place with God.

Your pause in the chaos.

Your reminder that you are not alone—and you don't have to carry life by yourself.

CHAPTER 6

Where Freedom Begins

Now that we have an understanding of the heart of the matter and the disconnection that broke us, I want to go a little deeper into the human experience and the bondage and suffering we face. I used to think freedom meant changing my behavior. Fixing what was broken. Doing better. Being better. I was spinning my wheels, trying to heal my soul with human logic. It wasn't working.

Just before beginning this book, I joined a coaching program called the 180 Method, which has been so beneficial in my healing journey. The 180 method describes us as *human beings* with two aspects.

- The **human**: our mind and soul.
- The **being**: our spirit, our divine essence, our connection to God.

The prisons we find ourselves in come from our human side (our soul) driven by our thoughts, emotions, and will, and a disconnection from our being. Therefore, healing requires us to reconnect with our being, where God resides. Where truth lives. That sacred place inside us that was never broken.

The program teaches that our human side is often ruled by the EGO, which stands for *Edging God Out.* But when we reconnect with our being, we invite God in. When EGO leads, it's a dead-end road; when we allow God to lead, His love fills us with a peace this world can't offer, no matter the circumstances we face.

While writing this book, I attended a training from Dr. Teneka called **"The Whole Man"** that mirrored much of what the 180 Method has revealed to me, with even greater clarity. She explained that we are **body, soul, and spirit**: three parts of one whole, each with its own role, each designed to be in harmony.

- **Our body** is connected to the world. It seeks comfort. It's motivated by pain and pleasure, reacting to the pull of what feels good and the push of what hurts.

- **Our soul** is connected to our self. It is the seat of our mind, will, and emotions; it's where our thoughts are formed, decisions are made, and feelings rise and fall. The soul drives us to produce, but it also craves rest. It carries our core needs: to be seen, heard, known, and loved. When these needs are met, they foster wholeness; when they're not, they create disruption and dysfunction. Much of the suffering we face is the cry of a soul that has grown exhausted.

- **Our spirit** is connected to the Godhead. It is where our relationship with God is established, where our true identity and divine purpose are imparted. It's our conscience, our intuition, and the place where communion with God happens. The spirit is where we receive truth, and where the truth of who we are—whole, beloved, redeemed—resides, untouched by the world's wounds.

To put this all together, imagine a car. Your body is the engine and frame. Your soul is the driver—thinking, feeling, and reacting. And your spirit is the navigation system—the GPS, the internal controls—that provides direction, truth, and purpose. Here's the key: the driver can't navigate well without the internal controls and GPS. The spirit was always designed to lead first, informing the soul where to go. When all three align—the spirit guiding, the soul responding, and the body carrying it out—the ride is steady, grounded, and purposeful. But when the GPS (our spirit) is shut off or ignored, the driver (our soul) panics, overcorrects, then tries to take control and "guess" which way to go on their own. The journey becomes chaotic, and we lose touch with our direction, our purpose, and ultimately, who we are.

When our **spirit**, the part of us that connects directly with God, takes the lead, the body and soul can come into alignment. This is where our purpose, direction, and truth is found. This is where peace settles in. This is where freedom begins.

But here's the problem: most of us are living upside down. We're being ruled by our body's cravings and our soul's wounds instead of being led by the Spirit. We let emotions lead the way, fear steer the wheel, and past experiences shape the patterns we now call personality. But those patterns aren't who we are, they're survival scripts.

Paul names this exact tension in Galatians 5:1 when he says, *"It is for freedom that Christ has set us free. Stand firm, then, and do not let yourselves be burdened again by a yoke of slavery."* Freedom, according to Scripture, is not something we achieve — it's something we **maintain by alignment**.

Paul goes on to describe two opposing forces at work within us: the flesh and the Spirit. This isn't about "bad behavior versus good behavior." It's about **what is leading**. The flesh represents life driven by self-effort, survival instincts, wounded desire, and fear. The Spirit represents life led by God's presence within us — truth, love, wisdom, and restraint flowing from relationship, not control.

Here's what's crucial: Paul doesn't say the flesh disappears when we come to Christ. He says the conflict remains — *but we now have a choice.*

"Walk by the Spirit," he writes, "and you will not gratify the desires of the flesh."

That word *walk* matters. It implies movement. Daily steps. Moment-by-moment decisions. Freedom is not lost in one dramatic fall; it's slowly surrendered when we stop paying attention to who is leading.

The flesh is loud. It reacts. It demands immediate relief. It is driven by cravings, emotions, old wounds, and the need to feel safe or soothed. The Spirit is quieter. It invites rather than forces. It leads us toward life even when it costs us comfort.

This is why freedom doesn't begin with behavior modification — it begins with **discernment**. With the simple but powerful question: *What is driving me right now?*

When the Spirit leads, the fruit is unmistakable: love, peace, patience, self-control, clarity, and life. When the flesh leads, even "good" actions eventually produce exhaustion, striving, comparison, and shame.

Paul's invitation is not to fight harder — it's to **yield more deeply**. To stop outsourcing leadership to fear, impulse, or old survival patterns, and to return authority to the Spirit of God within us.

This is where freedom is guarded.

Not by willpower.

Not by perfection.

But by choosing — again and again — who gets the lead.

When we were wounded, whether by rejection, trauma, neglect, betrayal, shame, grief—something fractured in us. The soul, designed to respond to the Spirit, started reacting to pain (the body) instead. We developed beliefs like *"I'm not enough," "People can't be trusted,"* or *"God is distant."* Those beliefs became thoughts. Those thoughts became automatic. And now they feel like the truth, even when they're not.

This is how the enemy works. He doesn't just tempt you with sin, he plants seeds of deception in the soil of your pain. Over time, if we don't interrupt the pattern, those lies grow into strongholds. But here's the truth that sets you free: **your spirit was made to lead.** When you surrender your life to Christ, your spirit is revived. And through that revival, you now have access to the mind of Christ (1 Corinthians 2:16).

You don't have to live in emotional chaos or mental torment. You can renew your mind, but it won't happen just by reading the Word. It happens when the Spirit of God breathes on it. Renewal is a spiritual process. It's not about striving, it's about surrender.

Romans 12:2 says, *"Be transformed by the renewing of your mind, so that you may prove what is the good, acceptable, and perfect will of God."* That word *prove* means to discern by the Spirit; to recognize truth as truth. And that only happens when the Spirit leads the soul, and the soul instructs the body.

The soul was never meant to lead, it was meant to produce. Your thoughts, your feelings, your will, they matter. But they were designed to follow the Spirit, not fight against it. Emotions are signals, not steering wheels. They inform, but they shouldn't rule.

The body? It screams for comfort, for control, for escape. But when the Spirit is empowered, even the body comes into submission. You wake up and say, *"I don't feel like praying,"* and the Spirit whispers, *"But you're not led by how you feel. You're led by who you are."*

And who are you? You are a child of God. You are whole in Christ. You have the mind of Christ. You have access to truth. You have the power to renew. And so, you take action anyway with that truth in mind.

When we experience struggle or thought loops and feel like there's no way out of it, we have to start with awareness. With stillness. With asking, *"Who's speaking right now? Is it my fear? My flesh? My old wound? Or is it the Spirit of God?"*

When the Lord speaks, it will feel like freedom. It will feel like love. Even when He convicts, there's no shame, only invitation. So if what you're hearing or feeling is laced with guilt, shame, panic, or condemnation, it's not God. It's either your soul, your body, or the enemy. And you have the authority to say *I reject that.* This is the habit we have to get into every single day to experience freedom.

So let me ask you:

1. What part of you has been leading?
2. Have your emotions been calling the shots?
3. Has your body been driving the decision?
4. Have your thoughts been rehearsing old lies?

It's time to come back into alignment with **Spirit as the lead. Then the Soul and Body can follow.** Because this is where freedom begins; not when life gets better, but when truth gets louder. When the Spirit gets access. When your heart returns home.

CHAPTER 7

Testimonies That
Tear Down Prison Walls

Testimonies of struggle and rising are sacred because they connect us to one another. They remind us that we're not alone. In the telling and the listening, something holy happens: our shared humanity is sanctified.

Throughout these pages, I will share parts of my own story alongside the stories of others who have walked through their own prisons—some literal, others invisible—and discovered freedom, whether in the midst of the mess or on the other side of it. Together, we will explore prisons of addiction, incarceration, religious wounding, financial hardship, and mental captivity, including Brooke's journey through postpartum psychosis and a severe physical illness that left her a prisoner in her own body. It's through the telling of these stories that hearts are restored and hope is ignited.

Some stories you'll read are of people who have already come through their prison doors. Others are still wrestling, still rising. But it doesn't matter where you are in the process. Freedom can break in at any moment, under any circumstance, even in the most unlikely of places.

For those behind literal bars, freedom may never come externally. But that doesn't mean your soul can't be set free. Because as you've seen by now, true freedom isn't about what's happening outside you, it's about what's happening within you. It's through testimonies that we connect in a tangible way to the truth that healing is possible, freedom is real, and no matter how dark it gets, there is always a way through.

And so, before I share the stories of others, I want to pause and let you into more of mine. Because every page of this book was born not just from theory and professional experience, but from lived experience; through battles fought, prisons endured, and grace discovered in the midst of it all. My journey, like everyone else's, is far from perfect, but it's proof that even in the mess, God can write redemption.

***

From as far back as I can remember, I've always had a heart for the hurting and a love for the lost. It wasn't something taught, it was something I felt deep in my soul. I was drawn to people's struggles and longed to bring love and compassion to those places. It was as if their pain spoke a language only my heart could understand.

When I reflect on the earliest moments that shaped my purpose, I'm brought back to memories with my best friend's sister, Becky. A little girl with severe cerebral palsy. She couldn't walk, talk, or eat on her own. When I met her, she was just four years old, spending her days in a crib, fed through a tube, her tiny body often wracked by seizures. While many might have overlooked her, I was drawn to her. I saw her. I didn't see her prison or her limitations. I saw her light.

When I'd visit my friend's house, my twin sister would run off to play, but I would go straight to Becky. I'd sit beside her crib, talking to her, just being with her. She was an incredible soul. Though we couldn't communicate in the traditional sense, our souls spoke fluently. Through that unspoken language, we formed a special bond.

Her mother, a woman of unshakable faith, had a way of making even the hardest moments feel tender. When Becky had seizures, she would excitedly say, *"Where you running to, baby girl?"*, as if her daughter were chasing dreams instead of being caught in something beyond her control. At the time, my child's heart believed Becky really was running in her sleep. It wasn't until I was older that I fully understood the depth of her mother's love. When Becky passed away at just six years old, my ten-year-old heart shattered in a way I didn't yet have the language for. She left an imprint on my soul that will never fade.

That same friend's family had close friends who fostered children, opening their home to kids in need. I remember being captivated by their kindness, their unwavering faith, and their ability to create a place of belonging. Something deep stirred in me. I wanted those children to know how loved and seen they were. That experience planted a seed, one that grew into my desire to pursue social work. I wanted to help children in foster care find the love and stability they deserved.

My mom also played a big part in shaping my heart. She often took us to volunteer, including at the Special Olympics each year. But what left the deepest mark was our time at Warren Village, a transitional housing program for single parents rebuilding their lives. I remember the families we met, not as strangers, but as warriors. They were doing the hard work of healing and surviving, and every time I stepped into that space, something inside me said, *This is what you're here for.* My soul felt at home.

Looking back, these were quiet whispers directing my path, guiding me toward a purpose I couldn't fully see yet. From the very beginning, I was called to walk alongside the bound and the broken. To bring light to the darkest places. To remind people, even in their suffering, that they are deeply loved and seen.

We all struggle in one way or another, and I've always carried a deep heart for our shared humanity, no matter how different our stories may seem. Even as a child, I knew this to be true: real, unconditional love has the power to heal. We are all created in the image of God, and our purpose is to become more like Him. As I reflect on my life and where I am today, it's clear that I am here–part of God's army—to be the hands and feet of Jesus, working His love and light through me and into the world so that every soul I meet will know they are seen, loved, and worthy.

I remember the first time I personally felt like a prisoner in my own mind. I was ten years old when I developed severe Obsessive-Compulsive Disorder. It began to interfere with my daily life and functioning. My twin sister used to get migraines, and I became terrified that if she touched me, I'd get one too. I began tying and untying my shoes until it "felt right." I'd open and close doors repeatedly until I could move on. I felt trapped inside my own fears, stuck in mental loops I couldn't escape.

My parents got me into a child psychologist, and everything changed when she finally gave what I was experiencing a name. She explained that I had OCD and showed me what it looked like in the brain. Then she said something that changed everything: *"You can totally overcome this. We just have to teach your brain that everything it's worrying about is false and that you are safe."*

Those words gave me hope. From that moment on, I committed to following everything she taught me. The road wasn't quick or easy, but over the course of two years and without medication, I was able to overcome the OCD. For the first time in what felt like forever, I experienced freedom. That freedom became the first of many *plot twists* where healing began to rewrite the narrative of my life. But like all the best stories, life circled back with another unexpected twist— one that would once again leave me a prisoner in my own mind.

In my early twenties, I found myself in another mental prison; this time, anxiety came back with a vengeance. It was 2008, and I was consumed by relentless panic. I could barely leave my house. I was diagnosed with agoraphobia and panic disorder. The panic attacks were suffocating, trapping me in a fear I couldn't outrun. At my lowest, I reached a place of despair where it was the closest I'd ever come to having thoughts of suicide. I remember thinking, *I can't live the rest of my life like this.* It was dark. Isolating. Paralyzing.

But I stayed in the fight, one day at a time.

Therapy helped. But one book in particular—*Anxiety Free* by Robert Leahy—was life-changing. It gave me practical tools to retrain my brain, face my fears, and rebuild my sense of safety. With time, effort, and a willingness to confront the discomfort (that is one essential piece to healing), the grip of anxiety began to loosen.

It was a long road. A lonely road. One that took a couple of years to walk. But eventually, the cave turned and I began to see light again. Today, aside from the occasional "typical anxiety," I can honestly say I am anxiety-free. And I credit Leahy's book as a pivotal turning point. Books can change lives. Sometimes they come at the exact moment your story is begging for a plot twist. My prayer is that this book becomes that moment for you: your turning point. Your freedom.

More importantly, growing closer to God again has broken fear's hold on me in a way nothing else ever could. Fear is not from God. And the more grounded and surrendered I am in His love, the more peace I feel. The more free I am.

Yet, life has a way of circling back with new battles just when you think you've finally found steady ground. Not long after emerging from the shadows of anxiety, another plot twist came—one I could never have prepared for.

I was diagnosed with Charcot–Marie–Tooth disease, a progressive neuromuscular condition that would eventually make walking and using my hands difficult. The neurologist explained that by my thirties, I would likely need braces to walk. There is no cure—only progression.

I remember asking whether diet or exercise could help. He told me no. Because it is a peripheral neuropathy, the nerves themselves become damaged; without proper nerve stimulation, the muscles weaken, waste away, and lose their strength.

I was just 22, when I received the diagnosis. For days, I lay numb in bed, imagining a future where I would no longer be able to walk without assistance. It was terrifying. Then something shifted. I made a choice: I would not become a **victim of my circumstances.** From that moment on, I focused on what I could control—eating well, exercising, and doing everything I could to keep my body strong for as long as possible. **The rest, I surrendered.**

It's remarkable what that mindset has led to. Now, at 37, I'm far from needing braces. I weight train five days a week and have even competed in fitness competitions. Through consistent exercise and healthy eating, I've reversed some symptoms and slowed the progression.

That doesn't mean the struggle is gone—my feet are numb, and I know the day will come when I'll need help walking. Still, I'm at peace. I'm doing everything I can to keep my body strong, and I'm trusting God with the rest. He has given me grace and strength—even in seasons when I wasn't searching for Him—to face each chapter so far. And I trust He will continue to carry me forward, one step at a time.

As you've seen by now, life has a way of continuing to take twists and turns we never saw coming. And the next ones would take me into the deepest valleys I'd ever walk. In 2018, I lost a dear friend to suicide; In 2020, my brother to an overdose. Then, in 2021, as I previously mentioned, I faced the unthinkable when I lost my student to suicide, and just seven days later, my son to fentanyl poisoning.

There are no words that can fully capture the weight of those losses. The grief came in waves—crashing over me, threatening to pull me under. And yet, even in the darkest nights, I discovered something surprising that I hadn't known before: freedom is not the absence of pain, but the presence of God in the middle of it.

His nearness became the lifeline I clung to when everything else slipped through my fingers. Step by step, breath by breath, He reminded me that freedom isn't reserved for easy seasons—it's found in the ones that break us open. Because freedom in Him isn't about what's happening around us; it's about what **He is doing within us.**

What God has done within me has been the real game-changer. And what He can do within you may be the freedom you never saw coming in your own story.

Right now, as I mentioned in the prologue, I'm walking through a messy financial prison—one I'll share more about in Chapter 14. And yet, I've learned this: every prison I've faced—mental (OCD, anxiety, fear), physical (chronic illness), emotional (grief), and now financial—has carried within it the possibility of soul-deep growth and transformation. As painful as the journey is, there has always been healing and greater peace on the other side.

I've come to see that the deeper the valley, the greater the rise that awaits.

I share these stories not to highlight my survival, but to remind you of yours. Your darkest moment may be the very place where your plot twist begins. It only takes an open, surrendered heart.

The prison is not the finale. It's the setup—the turning point that draws you closer to your purpose in Him.

CHAPTER 8

A Soul Set Free: Nate's Plot Twist

There are moments in life when a soul teeters between heaven and hell. Caught between death and deliverance. For Nate Bates, that moment wasn't metaphorical, it was literal. Twice.

His story isn't just one of addiction and recovery. It's a story of war: a war for his soul. And the one who claimed victory wasn't Nate. It was Jesus.

THE EARLY FRACTURE

Nate was born into a home that had everything it needed materially, but emotionally and spiritually there was a void. God wasn't present in the day-to-day, and a silent fracture ran through the walls of his childhood. His father favored his brother, leaving Nate to walk on eggshells—the tension between family members thick but unspoken. Beneath it all, Nate wrestled with a lingering question: "Why am I the outsider?"

That question was answered one day when Nate stumbled upon a hidden document on the family computer, a 13-page, single-spaced confession from his father. And in it, Nate read the unthinkable: every bad thing that had ever happened in his dad's life was, in his father's eyes, somehow because of Nate's birth.

It shattered him. At 13, he internalized a lie that would drive years of destruction: "If even my own dad doesn't want me, what's the point?"

That pain became rebellion. That wound became a weapon. And the enemy, a master at whispering lies into our pain, used it to keep Nate running from his worth, his identity, and ultimately, from God.

REBELLION IN THE NAME OF FREEDOM

Nate began drinking and smoking at 12. By 14, his father had been diagnosed with terminal lung cancer. Even though Nate had a negative view of his father, he was still his father. And watching him deteriorate, skeletal and medicated, only fueled Nate's anger. *If this is who God is*, Nate thought, *then I want nothing to do with Him*. He was middle fingers to the sky and a full-out rejection of anything holy.

And so began the chase for numbness, for adrenaline, for belonging. He dove headfirst into the rave scene, the drug culture, metaphysical philosophies, and anti-God rhetoric. He overdosed twice. He lived to party and planned to die young. His logic, reasoning, and identity were completely hijacked by addiction, and even deeper than that, the lies of the enemy. But beneath all that chaos, another war was brewing—an invisible one. And it was getting ready to surface.

THE FIRST OVERDOSE: SALVATION

One night, after a party filled with ecstasy, weed, and alcohol, Nate began to feel something terrifying. His soul was being pulled from his body; he could feel it. Tunnel vision overtook him, and he became hyper-aware of thousands of eager hands dragging his spirit down a dark spiral staircase. It wasn't poetic. It was real.

He grabbed his keys and, somehow in the middle of overdosing, drove a stick-shift truck three miles home. He called the only safe person he knew, his mother, just as she was about to leave church. Nate's mother had always carried quiet faith during his childhood years, handed down from a God-fearing grandfather.

"Mom . . . am I God?" he asked.

She dropped everything and rushed home. As she walked through the door, a light broke through the darkness. She grabbed her son and said, "Say it, Nathan. Say you love Jesus." In a tunnel of chaos, Nate said it: "I love Jesus."

And everything shifted.

It wasn't just emotional, it was spiritual. Paramedics arrived. Nate's heart was racing at 236 beats per minute. He fought off EMTs and police officers, threw grown men across the room, tore out of handcuffs. It was chaos in the physical realm, but even more so in the spiritual. He was fighting for his soul, and Jesus was fighting for him.

That night, Nate saw a cross illuminated in the hospital ceiling tiles. And in that moment, he knew: "Jesus, You're real."

That was the moment Nate experienced salvation, and it was a life-altering moment for him. But surrender? That would come later.

THE SECOND OVERDOSE: SURRENDER

After getting clean for 74 days, Nate relapsed. He thought he could handle a beer. Quickly, he found he couldn't. The spiral began again, and one night at a desert rave, a woman gave him pills in exchange for gas. Nate took them and immediately overdosed.

But this time, God didn't yank him back. Instead, God whispered, "I got you out of the first one. Now it's your turn." And in that overdose, Nate faced an ultimatum. As he asphyxiated, the war returned: the hands, the darkness, the suffocating weight of death.

But then came the Voice: "Choose today whom you will serve." Everything went still. And from a place deeper than words, Nate threw all his chips on the table of eternity. "God, I'm all in." From that point forward he said, "Wherever You want me to go, I'll go. Whatever You want me to do, I'll do." He had finally surrendered, and that would be the major turning point in Nate's life. A plot twist that would lead him to freedom through Christ.

INTO THE WILDERNESS

In this place of surrender, God led Nate to a place he never imagined, a recovery ranch in Southern California called Calvary Ranch.

Nothing made logical sense for him to go to this place, but that is where God directed him to go, and being that he was in full surrender with God now, he left school, comfort, and everything he knew. Through his time on the ranch, he learned how to care for animals, to serve with humility, and to build a relationship with Jesus in silence and sweat. He lived alongside other men who were broken, healing, and hungry for freedom. And it was there, in solitude and surrender, that Nate truly began to heal.

He would sit on the altar of the sanctuary, in front of a crown of thorns made by the ranch founder, and weep—not from pain, but from gratitude. "Who am I," he'd ask, "that You know me? That You love me like this?" In that moment, Nate experienced the miracle of grace. A grace that doesn't just pull us from the pit. It meets us there, and walks us out.

SPIRITUAL WARFARE IS REAL

What Nate came to understand, through the overdose, the surrender, and the quiet of the ranch, is this: addiction isn't just a mental or physical issue. It's spiritual.

Satan doesn't show up with horns. He shows up with a lie: "Do what you want. Live your truth. There is no cost." But the cost is real. And Nate saw it clearly with spiritual eyes. He fought demons, literally. He battled spirits. He saw darkness. But more importantly, he saw light. And he saw the power of Jesus over all of it.

Recently, Nate joined me on my podcast, *Soul Soldier Speaks*, and shared a simple yet powerful prayer he begins each day with: **"God, get in my head before I do."** That line stopped me in my tracks. It stirred something deep in my spirit, a holy nudge from God to go deeper, right here in these pages, into the spiritual warfare we're all facing. Because I've seen it up close.

You see, we often think of heaven and hell as distant places beyond this life. But they're not. I've come to believe that Jesus wants to save us now, to get Heaven *into* us now, while we're still living, still breathing, still in the fight. And I've come to know, with aching clarity, that many people are living in hell right here on Earth.

These aren't just "destinations" beyond the physical world. They are present realities. But here's the good news: We have a choice. Are we going to follow the light or keep believing the lies of the enemy and falling into the dark? The light that saves and restores is available to us at any point at any time. We just have to open up to it.

And this is why it matters to discuss spiritual warfare. To overcome the battles raging in and around us, we first have to understand them. We need to recognize the war we're in, learn how to suit up for it, and most importantly, remember that the ultimate victory has already been won.

Freedom is possible. Even in the darkest of places. Even in the middle of the storm. In the chapters ahead, we'll dive deeper into this spiritual battle, the one often waged not with chains or bars, but in the quiet battlefield of the mind. Because that's where the enemy loves to start. If he can get you to believe a lie, he doesn't need to imprison your body. You'll live like it's true . . . even if it's killing you.

But there's a plot twist. Truth always gets the final word.

This is the battle Nate had to face when he decided to get sober. It wasn't just the battle of addiction, it was the battle of identity. For so long, he believed he was the problem. He was unlovable. That life was happening to him, not for him. That freedom was for other people, not him.

But then something shifted. Nate didn't just find sobriety. He found salvation. And when he did, he realized the war wasn't over, it had just entered a new arena. A spiritual one.

"Once I accepted Jesus, that's when the spiritual battle really began."

It wasn't just about resisting temptation. It was about retraining his mind; it was about recognizing the lies he'd believed and replacing them with truth. The real battle, he said, was spiritual warfare. And it was intense.

He started showing up for church every weekend. Getting into God's Word. Praying daily. And most importantly, he began putting on the full armor of God. Not just metaphorically, but intentionally. Daily. Nate knew this wasn't just recovery. It was a battle that he needed to suit up for every day with protection.

HIS WAY REDEMPTION RANCH

Today, Nate has begun to answer the calling God has placed on his heart that he has been running from for over a decade. Nate finally said yes to starting His Way Redemption Ranch: a Christ-centered recovery ranch located in Arizona currently in the start up phases. This is a place where men will experience the kind of transformation Nate did. Not just sobriety, but freedom. Not just services, but Jesus.

It's not just a ranch. It's a battlefield for redemption. And as Nate puts it, "Even if only one soul is saved, it's worth it. Give me one."

Nate should've died—twice. By every statistic, every standard, every logical conclusion, he should've been a casualty of addiction. But God.

The plot twist wasn't that Nate survived. The plot twist was that Jesus rewrote the ending. And now, through building His Way Redemption Ranch, Nate, through the redeeming love and freedom of Jesus, can help others rewrite theirs. Because no matter how far you've gone, how broken you are, or how many overdoses, relapses, or lies you've believed . . . there is a way out.

His name is Jesus. And the door is already open.

CHAPTER 9

Freedom in the Fight

As you've likely begun to see, there's a war happening, and most people don't even realize it. It's not fought on distant battlefields or broadcast in breaking news. It's fought in hearts. In minds. In families. In prisons, both visible and invisible. It's spiritual. And it's real.

Before we move into more testimonies of people who have found freedom, whether in the middle of their mess or on the other side, we need to pause. We need to look closer at the spiritual warfare we first got a glimpse of in Nate's story. Because if we don't understand the battle we're in—the one raging around us and within us—we'll never fully grasp the freedom that's available to us.

We often shy away from the topic. The words *spiritual warfare* make some people think of sensationalized movies or over-the-top imagery. But according to the Bible, there is a very real enemy, a dark force actively working to "steal, kill, and destroy" (John 10:10). His battleground is often your mind, your identity, your purpose, and your peace. This isn't just a church concept or a dramatic metaphor. It's the invisible war that shapes your thoughts, directs your choices, and tries to keep you bound.

In this chapter, we're going to expose the lies of the enemy and learn how to fight back with the truth of the gospel. And here's the good news, as Pastor Chad Moore says, *"We don't fight for victory, we fight from it."* [1]

That truth was the heartbeat of a sermon series at Sun Valley Community Church called *Battle Ready*, a message tailor-made for every human being who knows what it feels like to be in a fight, which is all of us, because none of us get through life unscathed. Whether you're locked behind physical bars or imprisoned in the many other ways we've discussed, the path to freedom begins with learning how to stand firm.

The battle isn't always visible. There's a physical world we can see and a spiritual world we often can't. But just because we don't see it doesn't mean it's not shaping us. Scripture makes it clear: "We wrestle not against flesh and blood, but against . . . spiritual forces of evil in the heavenly realms" (Ephesians 6:12).

And the enemy doesn't need to destroy your body if he can deceive your mind. His primary weapon isn't a sword, it's a story. An accusation. An ideology meant to convince you that your prison is permanent. He'll try to chain you to old labels:

- *Addict*

- *Failure*

- *Unworthy*

- *Too far gone*

And whether you have a spiritual belief system or read scripture or not, we've all experienced the battle. But just as real as the battle is, so is the victory. And God reveals the truth of who we are: chosen, loved, redeemed, which is a direct threat to the enemy's plans. That's why the Apostle Paul tells us to "put on the full armor of God" (Ephesians 6:11). Not to hide from the fight, but to stand in it. Without the armor, we're exposed. With it, we are unshakable.

The armor is not optional. Ephesians 6:10–13 tells us to "be strong in the Lord and in His mighty power" and to "put on the full armor of God, so that you can take your stand against the devil's schemes." Let that sink in: it's *His* mighty power, not yours. Not your willpower. Not your good behavior. Freedom doesn't come from trying harder, it comes from surrendering deeper to the one who can see what we can't see. Victory is not about self-help; it's about Spirit-help. That's what grace is. That's what the armor is for. This was the pivotal turning point in Nate's recovery. He began putting on the full armor of God, daily. The belt of truth. The breastplate of righteousness. The shoes of peace. The shield of faith. The helmet of salvation. The sword of the Spirit.

THE BELT OF TRUTH

Every prison starts with a lie. Every freedom starts with the truth. In the Garden of Eden, the enemy didn't swing a sword, he asked a misleading question: "Did God really say . . .?" (Genesis 3:1). That's why Satan's lies are so dangerous. One distorted thought can wreck a whole life.

As Pastor Robert Watson shared in the second message of Sun Valley's *Battle Ready* series, the spiritual war inside us isn't just about what we do, it's about what we believe [2]. If the enemy can plant a lie and get us to build our life around it, he doesn't need chains. We'll stay imprisoned on our own. And that's why truth is our first line of defense. If lies imprison us, truth is what sets us free (John 8:32).

When Paul wrote about the armor of God, the first piece he mentioned was the belt of truth (Ephesians 6:14). This wasn't just a piece of fabric. It was the foundation that held a Roman soldier's armor together. It secured the sword, stabilized the body, and prepared the warrior for combat.

In the same way, truth is what holds us steady. But here's the question we each have to answer: What belt are you wearing? Pastor Robert brought things from home with a striking illustration: a construction belt, a police belt, a karate black belt, a rodeo belt, and a championship wrestling belt. Each one signaled what kind of battle its wearer was stepping into.

Pastor Robert shared a moment from his visit to Florence West Prison in Arizona. He noted that many had believed a lie that led them behind bars. But now, through Jesus, they are connecting to truth. And in truth, they are finding freedom [3].

He described listening to an older inmate sing a gospel song in the prison yard, surrounded by barbed wire but filled with peace and the presence of God. "In that moment," he said, "we weren't in prison, we were at church." Because freedom isn't about your surroundings. It's about your spirit. "Where the Spirit of the Lord is, there is freedom" (2 Corinthians 3:17).

THE BREASTPLATE OF RIGHTEOUSNESS

The Breastplate of Righteousness guards the heart, the place where unhealed wounds can harden into weapons. As we explored in the earlier chapter, *The Heart of the Matter*, everything flows from the heart. That's why true healing and lasting freedom begin when we address what's happening deep within, known as the "soul-heart".

The enemy knows this. That's why he targets the heart with lies designed to corrode it from the inside out. Lies about who you are, what you're worth, and whether you can be whole again. Without protection, those lies take root, and over time they can harden our hearts into something unrecognizable. That's why the breastplate matters. It is Christ's righteousness, not our own, that surrounds us and shields our most vulnerable places so shame, condemnation, and fear can't pierce through.

I think of Brooke, whose story you'll hear in a later chapter. She told me she'd take her visible, physical illness over her invisible mental illness any day. When her body was broken, people showed up. When her mind was broken, she fought alone. Her words are a sobering reminder that some of the deepest battles are unseen and often fought in isolation. But the breastplate reminds us: we are never actually fighting alone. We are covered. We are held. And when our own strength fails, His righteousness still stands guard over our heart.

THE SHOES OF PEACE

Roman soldiers wore sandals with spikes to hold their ground. They weren't made for retreat, they were made for standing up tall. They were made to confront the enemy with an unshakable strength. And there's something interesting when it comes to their spiky shoes—they weren't overtly visible like sharp swords and mighty shields. The spikes were there to quietly help each individual soldier in their quest for victory. Powerful, but not loud. And in our lives, there's another word that carries that same quiet power: peace.

As Pastor Chad said, *"Biblical peace is tranquility in the midst of trouble."* [4]

When Nate shared his story of addiction, relapse, and a radical encounter with Jesus, he described peace that didn't come after the storm, but in it. Standing in a prison yard of his own making, he felt the kind of grounding only God could give, a peace that held him steady when everything else was shaking. Peace is not passive, it's a weapon. It steadies you so you can move forward, carrying light into dark places.

And let's get honest, how many of us have searched for peace in a bottle, in applause, in people, in the endless scroll of things that never satisfy? We look outside ourselves, hoping to fix an inner ache. But the peace that holds in a storm doesn't come from the outside in, it comes from the inside out. From Spirit, to soul, to body. Not the other way around.

Jesus never promised a life without trouble. In fact, He said, "In this world you will have trouble." But He didn't stop there. He followed it with the promise that changed everything: "But take heart! I have overcome the world" (John 16:33). That's what gospel shoes remind us of. That even when our mind is a battlefield and our circumstances are heavy, we can stand in the victory already won.

When I was in the thick of my grief, I didn't need shallow positivity or cheap theology. I needed a peace that could hold me there, in the pit, in the pain, in the breaking. I needed shoes that wouldn't slip when the ground crumbled beneath me.

The gospel has given me that gift. And as I write this, I sit in awe that these words are being spoken through me because of where I started. But it's a truth that's slowly sinking in, resonating in the deepest parts of me: that I am loved, that I am chosen, that I am redeemed by a Savior who didn't wait for me to clean up before coming to Him but met me right in the middle of my mess—and not only met me, but pulled out all the stops to get me to notice Him.

Peace is not a vibe. It's a weapon. And it's meant to be released, not just received. Gospel peace doesn't just hold you steady, it sends you into battle, to bring light to the dark places, to love those the world forgets, to storm the gates of hell with the authority of heaven. Jesus said the gates of hell won't prevail. So maybe today, your first move isn't to run, it's to stand. To let the gospel ground you, steady you, fill you. Then, with that same peace you've received, go. Go love the one who's still trapped in chaos. Go forgive the one who wounded you. Go serve, go speak, go fight with love and light. Your life won't be the same, in the absolute best way.

Put on your shoes, warrior. The world doesn't need more noise. It needs people who walk in peace, grounded, ready, moved by the Spirit, not the storm. The battle is already won. But we still have ground to take.

THE SHIELD OF FAITH

And just when you find your footing, here come the arrows. Can you relate? They look like bills you can't pay, fights you can't fix, memories you can't escape. But underneath it all, they're lies lit on fire. Paul writes, "Take up the shield of faith, with which you can extinguish all the flaming arrows of the evil one" (Ephesians 6:16).

In his sermon, *Obeying God When It Doesn't Make Sense*, Pastor Lucas Cooper said, *"You already have exactly what you need to eradicate, annihilate, and obliterate all fear in your life."* [5] And when your arms are too tired to hold your shield, you lock it with someone else's. That's what faith in community looks like.

Pastor Lucas outlined three ways to wield the shield of faith, just as Jesus did in the wilderness: gratitude, truth, and worship.

- **Gratitude** shifts us into abundance, reminding us that, with God, we already have what we need. You can't live in lack and abundance at the same time. Gratitude is a shield that can protect us from misery and temptation.

- **Truth** lifts God's Word above our emotions and speaks it louder than the lies. The enemy doesn't just throw fear; he twists truth, convincing us that feelings are facts. But faith declares: God's Word is greater than my emotions. When the enemy tempted Jesus, He didn't react emotionally, He responded with Scripture. And so can we. Hold God's Word higher than your inner storm.

- **Worship** turns our eyes from fear to the One on the throne, shrinking the enemy's voice under the weight of His glory.

Faith was never meant to be held alone. Like Roman soldiers locking shields, we protect one another, lifting ours when a brother or sister is too weary to lift theirs. Fear isolates, but faith unites. The same God who was faithful then is faithful now. So pick up your shield. Lift it daily. Lock it with others. And watch faith extinguish fear, every time.

THE HELMET OF SALVATION

Some battles are loud and obvious. Others happen quietly, thought by thought, lie by lie, whisper by whisper. That's the kind of war the enemy loves most: a mental one, especially when you're in the messy middle between who you were and who you're becoming. You don't see it coming, and suddenly you're spiraling, wondering if you're loved, if you're enough, if you'll make it, if God's still with you, or if you've gone too far to come back.

The helmet isn't just to protect our skulls, it's to guard our souls from mental collapse. The battle doesn't always start with an explosion; sometimes it starts with a whisper. A single lie. A subtle doubt. If the enemy can infiltrate your mind, he doesn't need to chain your hands. A tormented mind will paralyze the body. If he can steal your peace, he'll stall your purpose, trapping you in cycles of overthinking, anxiety, shame, and fear until you forget who you are and what you're made for. The helmet of salvation anchors you in what is already true, what is being made true, and what is yet to come true.

Pastor Chad explained salvation in three parts:

- **Justification**: You have been saved. Paid in full.

- **Sanctification**: You are being saved. God is transforming you daily.

- **Glorification**: You will be saved. The battle will end. [6]

The helmet deflects the whispers that try to convince you of all the things you're not. It's like a quarterback's helmet tuning you into the voice of the coach who sees the whole field. God can see what we can't see, so we need His perspective and His words to cover and protect us on this battleground called life.

When life hits me the hardest, the helmet has become my lifeline, grounding my mind, covering my heart, and securing my soul in truth. What I've come to learn is that God's path will always feel like peace and freedom. The enemy's path feels like fear, doubt, and shame. The helmet protects us from the lies and fears of the enemy.

THE SWORD OF THE SPIRIT

The final piece of armor we have available to us is the Sword of the Spirit. Most of us walk into life's battles unarmed. We may think we're tough. Maybe we've survived a few fights, even come out on top once or twice. But as Pastor Robert Watson shared in the *Battle Ready* series, the moment we think we've got the fight figured out, life shows up with a bigger opponent. Suddenly we're flat on our backs, gasping for air, wondering what just hit us [7].

Paul reminds us in Ephesians 6 that our strength doesn't come from self-will or swagger—it comes from God. Then Paul names our one offensive weapon: "the sword of the Spirit, which is the word of God" (Ephesians 6:17). Hebrews 4:12 says it is "alive and active, sharper than any double-edged sword."

Pastor Robert explained that the Word works in three dimensions:

- **Graphē**: the written words on the page.

- **Logos**: the message and meaning.

- **Rhema**: the spoken Word declared aloud.

We all face battles, and the Word of God speaks to every one of them. First in scripture, then in voice. When we declare it over ourselves, our families, and our situations, we invite heaven's power into the fight.

For the lost: "He is patient . . . not wanting anyone to perish" (2 Peter 3:9).

For shame: "If anyone is in Christ, the new creation has come" (2 Corinthians 5:17).

For anxiety: "Do not be anxious about anything . . . present your requests to God" (Philippians 4:6).

For guilt: "If we confess our sins, He is faithful and just to forgive us" (1 John 1:9).

For fear: "The Spirit God gave us . . . gives us power, love, and self-discipline" (2 Timothy 1:7).

For marriage: "Submit to one another out of reverence for Christ" (Ephesians 5:21).

For feeling unloved: "How wide and long and high and deep is the love of Christ" (Ephesians 3:18–19).

Speak these truths in your heart, in your mind, and out loud. Let them cut through whatever lie is consuming you. When you declare Scripture, you're not repeating something old, you're enforcing something eternal. You're reminding your soul what's real. And you're choosing a plot twist the enemy didn't see coming: freedom.

Every time you declare truth in the face of a lie, you take back stolen ground. This is how captives walk free. This is how lies are dismantled. This is how the plot turns. So open your mouth. Raise your sword. Speak what's already been written.

Footnotes

This chapter was informed and inspired by the *Battle Ready* sermon series taught by Pastors Chad Moore, Robert Watson, and Lucas Cooper at Sun Valley Community Church. While I've woven my own voice and reflections throughout, the credit for the original teaching belongs to them. For the full *Battle Ready* series and teaching straight from their sermons, I encourage you to visit

https://www.youtube.com/@SunValleyCC

[1] Pastor Chad Moore, *Battle Ready: We Don't Fight for Victory, We Fight From It*, Sun Valley Community Church.

[2] Pastor Robert Watson, *Battle Ready: Belt of Truth*, Sun Valley Community Church.

[3] Pastor Robert Watson, *Battle Ready: Belt of Truth*, Sun Valley Community Church.

[4] Pastor Chad Moore, *Battle Ready: Peace in the Fight*, Sun Valley Community Church.

[5] Pastor Lucas Cooper, *Battle Ready: The Fear That Grips Us*, Sun Valley Community Church.

[6] Pastor Chad Moore, *Battle Ready: What You Focus On Is What You Move Toward*, Sun Valley Community Church.

[7] Pastor Robert Watson, *Battle Ready: Sword of the Spirit*, Sun Valley Community Church.

CHAPTER 10

Prison to Purpose:
Jason Smith's Plot Twist

The fire started long before Jason ever lit a match. It began in the brokenness of a family tree split at the roots, in a home where love was scarce and survival was everything. Jason Smith's story isn't a clean one, but honestly, whose is? Jason's story is jagged, raw, and hard to read in parts. But that's exactly what makes it powerful. Because through all the trauma, violence, drugs, abandonment, and cycles of incarceration, a quiet miracle was unfolding. One that would only make sense in hindsight.

Jason was born in North Hollywood in 1972, raised in Hawthorne, California by a single mom who had big dreams but carried bigger wounds. His father left when he was a baby, unable to handle city life after growing up on the Salt River Indian Reservation. Jason would barely know him, a ghost of a man whose absence left a crater in his soul.

His mother, a smart woman with certifications in cosmetology and medical terminology, was herself a product of rejection. Born out of wedlock during WWII, she was handed off to her grandmother and never truly mothered. That wound rippled forward, bleeding into how she raised Jason.

He was seven years old when the darkness started to show.

He set a palm tree on fire in an alley. Not because he wanted to destroy something, but because something inside him was already burning. It was the year his mom fell apart. The man she loved died suddenly of a heart attack in another woman's bed. She spiraled into the arms of the Hell's Angels (a motorcycle club; yet widely classified as a gang by law enforcement and intelligence agencies) and the bottle. Jason would come home from school to find strangers passed out on their couch—bikers, drugs, chaos. He learned early how to survive beatings, noise, and neglect.

By junior high, Jason's mother tried to pull him out of the madness. They moved to Riverside, California. For a brief time, she got sober. Life stabilized. But it didn't last. She disappeared, jumping trains with old friends who rode the rails, leaving Jason and his little brother to fend for themselves. One day just before high school, Jason came home and his little brother was gone. His mom explained that she couldn't take care of him so she sent him to live with a friend. That crushed Jason. His little brother was all he had and they were close. Jason had had enough.

He moved in with his Aunt Julie and was soon pulled into a gang on the west side of Riverside. They offered what he always longed for: belonging, protection, family. His loyalty came at a cost: gun violence, theft, jail, and a steady descent into addiction with Meth and Angel dust. He was shot three times throughout his life. Survived a drive-by with 73 bullets in his car and only one wound in his arm. God's hand was on him, even then.

Still, Jason didn't know how to get out. He didn't know there *was* a way out.

At nineteen, he landed in prison for the first time. He was looking at four strikes, enough to bury him for life. But his grandmother, the one person who believed in him, got a lawyer who struck three of them. He served time. Got out. Went right back. Over the next eighteen years, he cycled through nine prison terms, four parole violations, and countless nights numbing his pain in all the ways he knew how.

Somewhere in the chaos, he had children. He didn't raise them. He couldn't. He was distracted by the drug and gang life. Still, God was writing a bigger story.

In one of his final prison terms, a lifer pulled him aside and said, "I want you to think of me when you leave." Confused, Jason asked why. He proceeded to tell Jason, "You've got something in you, Gizmo. Don't come back here. You don't belong in this place. You come in and out like it's nothing. You've got a good heart and if I had your chance, I'd leave and never look back. So when you're out there I want you to think of me." That conversation planted a seed.

When Jason finally chose rehab over more prison time, he expected rules and routine. What he found was Jesus. He came for treatment and Jesus met him there. Not with shame. Not with rules. With love. Pure, undeserved, relentless love. In that place, Jason got baptized. He discovered he had the gift of tongues. He felt the power of the Holy Spirit. He didn't earn it. He didn't understand it. But it was real. It was healing.

After graduating, he got his first real job. Bought the car of his dreams, a 1973 Caprice Classic lowrider that felt like a symbol of dignity. But just as he began to rise, life punched him again. His mom died suddenly from acute methamphetamine poisoning. Jason found her lifeless in bed. Even with their rocky past, Jason's mom was his best friend.

Grief took hold. He spiraled again. Sold everything. Relapsed. Blew through his inheritance. Then one day, he found himself having another experience he would never forget. He was sitting across from a drug counselor named Mr. Hernandez. Jason didn't walk into that place feeling holy or chosen. He felt wrecked. Tired. Strung out. He showed up because he had to. There God would continue to meet him in his mess and whisper life-giving words through unexpected voices. Jason described the encounter:

He walked into the office and there Mr. Hernandez looked at him with a quiet seriousness and said, "Okay. All right."

Jason, confused, said, "Okay . . . all right what?"

Mr. Hernandez paused, then said words Jason would never forget: "The Lord just told me something."

Jason was caught off guard. "What did He tell you?"

The counselor leaned in. "He said . . . you've got the keys."

"The keys? Keys to what?" Jason said.

"To every door. You're holding the keys to unlock doors most people can't. The Lord told me you have a calling on your life. You're going to walk into dark places and bring the light. You're going to go where others won't, and you're going to bring hope."

Jason tried to make sense of what he was hearing. He didn't feel like a man with purpose. He felt like a man falling apart.

"I don't know exactly what your calling is," Mr. Hernandez continued. "But it's big. And things are going to change for you. But first, you've got to get off probation. And you've got to stay off the drugs."

Jason was honest. He didn't pretend. He told Mr. Hernandez he was deep in the mess. The cops had just raided his house, smashing sinks and tearing through his things. They told him straight up: *If you don't move, something's going to happen.* Even the mayor of Beaumont stopped him on the street.

"You need to leave," the mayor said. "You could live a good life here, but not if you keep doing what you're doing. I knew your mom. This is a small community. We knew you were coming."

Jason was stunned. *How the hell did they know I was coming?* he thought. What he didn't realize was that the feds had been watching him for a long time. While he was in prison, he had protection from the Mexican Mafia, but he didn't use drugs. He did his time, clean. It was only when he got out that he slipped again. Back into addiction. Back into dealing. He wasn't trying to build a criminal empire, he was just surviving and living life the only way he knew how. But every step forward led him further into darkness. And yet, those little nudges from God would stick with him. He didn't understand them fully at the time. But something in his soul knew it was true. God wasn't done with him.

Jason would go on to sell his mom's house. He paid off his child support so he could finally reinstate his driver's license. And oddly enough, that moment marked the beginning of another subtle shift and whisper from God.

He had been clean for 12 months at this point. One day, he had to appear for a probation hearing. He arrived at court at 8:00 a.m. sharp, expecting to be processed and sent on his way. He waited. And waited. Lunch came and went. By 4:00 p.m., an hour before the courthouse closed, he was still sitting there, the last name not yet called. Finally, a sheriff stepped out of the courtroom, glanced down the hallway, and locked eyes with Jason, still seated, still waiting. He turned back inside, then reemerged to summon him.

Jason walked into the courtroom, unsure of what to expect. The judge took his seat and called him forward.

"All right, Mr. Smith. Approach the bench," he said, and Jason stepped forward. "You know why you're here?"

Jason nodded. "Probation hearing."

"Yeah, well, you've got a violation on file," the judge said.

Jason was confused. "What? For what?"

"Your probation officer says you haven't been reporting to him personally."

"I was told five months ago I could report through the kiosk system," Jason said. "I get a ticket then leave."

The judge said, "Yeah . . . you're right. I believe you. I think your probation officer just doesn't like you. I think he wanted to see you fail so he could send you back."

Jason stood there, feeling defeated.

"I kept you here all day on purpose," the judge continued. "I've seen you before. You show up to court, and right before your name's called, you try to leave. That's how I knew you were guilty. But this time? You stayed. That tells me something, and I believe you're being honest."

Then the judge leaned in and said words that Jason would never forget. "Jason, you're done with California."

Jason did a double take. "What do you mean, I'm done?"

"The probation department told us you've been trying to transfer to Arizona. But Arizona doesn't take guys like you: parolees and probationers with a record like yours. We wanted you to finish your time here and have a clean slate. And now . . . you do."

He continued, "You paid off your child support. You discharged your parole. Now I'm going to discharge your probation."

Then the judge's tone grew more serious. "But I need to warn you. Many guys your age don't get this chance. As many times as you've been in prison and who you run around with, you know exactly who I'm talking about: your 'big dogs'. You're lucky you were never validated in prison."

("Validated" generally refers to the process where prison officials officially designate an inmate as a gang member or affiliated with a Security Threat Group (STG), which can have significant consequences.)

Jason nodded, unsure of where this was going..

"You're getting a second chance in life," the judge said. "And if you really want it, we're going to give it to you. But you have to want it. This is your last warning. If you pick up another felony, the federal government will give you 45 years. You'll be labeled a habitual criminal. This is your last warning, so if you want this second chance in life, take it."

Then the judge stamped the paperwork, looked him in the eye, and said, "All right, Mr. Smith. I don't ever want to see you in my courtroom again. Have a nice life. Case closed."

Jason walked out with tears in his eyes. So much was running through his mind: grief, gratitude, disbelief. A door had opened. But he wasn't quite ready to walk through it. He stayed in California for nearly another year. By then, he was sleeping in a friend's trailer, still clinging to the familiar, unsure of what came next.

Then, one morning, he heard someone calling his name. He stepped outside and followed the voice toward a fence. There, over the fence, stood Linda, a friend of his younger brother's. A woman of deep faith. A woman who didn't just believe in God, she *listened* to Him.

Jason looked down at her. "Hey, what's up, Linda?"

She didn't hesitate. "God sent me here," she said. "It's time."

"Time for what?" Jason asked.

"It's time for you to go to Arizona."

Jason furrowed his brow. "Excuse me?"

"You've got to go. God said it's time for you to leave. That's all I can tell you. I love you. Bye."

And with that, she got in her car and drove off, down the alley, out of sight.

Jason stood there, stunned. And two weeks later, the girl he was seeing at the time pulled up and said, "Let's go to Arizona."

He looked at her, confused yet again. "What? How do you even know about that?"

"Linda told me to take your ass to Arizona."

Jason didn't need any more signs. It was time. He headed to Arizona in July of 2015.

He started working for his tribe, helping build a water treatment plant. He stayed with family for a while and then got his own apartment. The road would continue to be bumpy for many years thereafter.

Perhaps the most powerful moment of Jason's journey, one he hadn't spoken about much until recently, came after another devastating fall. After losing his daughter, Sabrina, to overdose on September 30, 2019, Jason spiraled hard. The grief was unbearable. He turned again to meth to cope, and the girl he was living with at the time was using too. The pain and rage that lived inside him began to boil over, and in early 2020, just as the world shut down for COVID, everything unraveled.

One day, after a heated argument turned physical, Jason walked out of the house in a storm of confusion and despair. And not far down the road on the reservation, he was surrounded by five Salt River Police vehicles. They told him to sit down, but he refused. One of the officers fired a 20-caliber block gun, striking Jason in the kneecap. He collapsed in the street, was rushed into surgery, and then booked into Salt River Jail, where he would spend the next year behind bars.

When he got out, he tried to do the right thing. He was clean for a time, working, trying to keep steady. But the woman he returned to hadn't changed. The chaos returned, and so did the drugs. After a few months, he left that relationship and moved in with his nephew. He started going back to church and even experienced deliverance at a Sunday night service. Deliverance is when God lifts a burden or breaks a stronghold in someone's life—and it can happen during worship, prayer, a moment of surrender and a variety of other ways.

But the next morning, the enemy came knocking. Jason relapsed again, just hours after being delivered. Still, God wasn't done. That Monday morning, Jason showed up for work through a day labor program with the tribe, assigned to maintenance at Talking Stick Golf Course. It was early, before dawn. As the sun began to rise over the mountains, Jason stood alone on holes 1 through 4, working in the stillness of morning.

Then something incredible and hard to make sense of happened. Jason heard a voice: "Look up." When Jason lifted his eyes to the sky, he saw something that would forever change him. In the clouds, formed in one massive shape, was a face: half Jesus, wearing a crown of thorns, and half lion. The image was clear; alive. And then he heard the voice again. "Get on your knees." He dropped to the sand in the trap he'd been cleaning, shaking, crying, overwhelmed. The Lord spoke to him in that moment: "Why do you defile your body? I pulled those demons out of you. Why do you defile the temple I made? Don't you know who I am? I am who I am. I called you to a path of righteousness, peace, and love."

Jason wept in the sand. "I'm sorry," he said through tears. "I'm sorry."

Then the voice said, "Get up." So he did, trembling. He got into his golf cart and drove to the next hole. But the voice wasn't done. As he arrived at the next sand trap, he heard it again: "Get on your knees." Jason obeyed. Again, he wept. Again, he shook. And then the sky opened.

As far as his eyes could see, across the horizon, the clouds parted into a line of angels: shoulder to shoulder, radiant and fierce. And then, riding above them, he saw Jesus on a white horse, a red sash across His chest, holding a sword high in the air. The horse stood on two legs, majestic and powerful.

Jesus spoke.

"Tell them I'm coming. Tell them who I am. I redeemed you. I forgive you. Tell them your story."

Then He gave Jason an instruction: "Go home. Go to the Arizona Deliverance Center in Phoenix. Get deliverance. And do not defile My temple ever again."

Jason rushed to his boss, still crying. When his boss asked what happened, Jason could barely form the words. "I can't work," he said. "I have to go." His boss, confused, simply nodded. "Go ahead." Jason went straight home. Then to the Arizona Deliverance Center. There, on June 27, 2022, he received full deliverance. And since that day, Jason has remained clean.

When Jason shared this with me, he said only a few people have heard this story. He said many would find it hard to believe. But Jason knows what he saw. He knows who he heard. He knows what he felt, and that was the final plot twist that set Jason on his path to true freedom and recovery.

Jason began sharing his story and serving in treatment centers. He attends church regularly along with men's bible studies.

His kids are still distant. His past still echoes. He still mourns the daughter he lost to overdose. He still misses the father he never got to know. But Jason is free now. Not because life is perfect, but because he finally gave Jesus the wheel.

"Every time I tried to drive my life, I wrecked it," Jason says. "But when I let Jesus lead, something shifts. Even when it's hard, I've got Jesus to lead the way. That's freedom."

It's a divine paradox: the more we try to control our lives, the more enslaved we become. But when we **surrender**, when we release control, pride, pain, addiction, identity, revenge, and self-will, we find a freedom that doesn't depend on our surroundings. That's because true freedom is not circumstantial—it's spiritual.

In Matthew 16:24–25 (NIV), Jesus said to his disciples, "Whoever wants to be my disciple must deny themselves and take up their cross and follow me. For whoever wants to save their life will lose it, but whoever loses their life for me will find it.'" Here, Jesus makes it clear: real life, **real freedom**, comes not from holding on, but from letting go. Surrender is the gateway to life change.

In 2 Corinthians 3:17 (NIV) (which I mentioned in an earlier chapter), when Paul is in prison, he describes experiencing freedom even behind bars.

He says, "Now the Lord is the Spirit, and where the Spirit of the Lord is, there is freedom."

Then Paul wrote this while under persecution. Later, in chains, he said, "I am in chains for Christ. . . and because of my chains, most of the brothers and sisters have become confident in the Lord."-Philippians 1:13–14 (NIV)

Despite his literal imprisonment, Paul radiated a freedom the world couldn't comprehend, because he had surrendered his entire life to Christ. He wasn't free **from** prison, but he was free **in** it.

And finally, it is important to note that surrender makes room for transformation. In Romans 12:2 (NIV) it says, "Do not conform to the pattern of this world, but be transformed by the renewing of your mind."

This transformation—freedom from old thinking, old habits, shame, self-hatred—only happens when we lay our lives down before God. Surrender opens the door for Him to do what we could never do on our own.

Contrary to what we may believe about surrender, it is not weakness. It's not giving up or giving in like it might sound. It's wisdom. It's choosing to stop walking with the enemy, to stop resisting God, to stop managing everything in our own strength, and let the One who made us lead us to the truth of who we are and the calling on our life.

In Jason's story, freedom didn't begin when he got clean, left prison, or moved to Arizona. It began when he said yes to the deeper surrender, to the idea that he wasn't in control, and that Christ was not only able, but willing, to carry what he couldn't. True freedom doesn't come when the cell door swings open, it comes when your soul bows to the One who opens every door.

And maybe that's the greatest plot twist of all. You don't need to be clean to come to Jesus. You don't need to have your relationships in order. You don't need to erase your past. You don't need to be outside the prison walls. You just need to be willing.

Jason became willing. But Jason's life didn't suddenly become picture-perfect. This is no Hallmark movie with a neat little bow. His past is still complicated. His relationships with his kids are strained or absent. His brother is homeless.

Redemption doesn't always look like restored circumstances. Sometimes it looks like a man finally learning how to forgive himself. Sometimes it looks like using our pain to set someone else free. Sometimes it looks like staying sober when everything in you wants to run.

Jason now walks in that kind of freedom, the kind Jesus gives in the middle of the mess. God is now using him to go into places most people won't go and bring light. He knows the streets. He knows the pain. And now he knows the way out. He serves in treatment centers. He shows up with love where darkness used to rule. He shares his testimony not as a polished man, but as a soul set free. A man once called Gizmo on the yard, now called chosen by God.

He'll tell you he's still in process. He gets grouchy. He struggles with grief. He longs to be the father he never had. But he'll also tell you this:

"Freedom isn't waiting for everything in your life to be fixed. Freedom is found in Christ, right in the middle of your brokenness."

Jason's story is not over. And neither is yours. We serve a God who writes plot twists no one saw coming. From prison to purpose. From addiction to anointing. From "never enough" to "my grace is sufficient."

No matter what prison you find yourself in, whether behind bars, trapped in addiction, haunted by shame, or crushed by the weight of your past, there is a way out. His name is Jesus. And the door is already open. He's just waiting for you to open your heart and step through it.

When I asked Jason what message he would give to someone currently in the middle of their mess, needing hope, he said he would tell them, "Jesus loves you," and, "He's the way, the truth, the life. If you just open your heart to Him and try to understand that you are loved more than anything in the world . . . it changes everything."

He went on to share how present the Lord has been in his life. How he's witnessed things that can't be explained: encounters with both angels and demons. And now, after everything, he looks back at what he's been through with gratitude. Gratitude that he's still here, still breathing. That he made it through. That he can sit down, heart open, and say,

"My name is Jason, and this is my story."

A story of survival.

A story of surrender.

A story of grace.

A story of a man whose life remains imperfect and finds freedom anyway.

Dope to Freedom: Jason Rudeen's Plot Twist

Some stories come at you like a freight train—raw, relentless, impossible to look away from. Jason Rudeen's life was one of those stories. From the outside, it might look like a trail of destruction—addiction, trauma, broken relationships, near-death moments—but underneath was a soul that refused to quit. His journey is not about glamorizing the chaos or shaming the mistakes; it's about the power of surrender, the grit it takes to fight for your life, and the grace of a God who steps into the mess and redeems what looked beyond saving.

Jason's path to freedom was not a straight line. It was littered with relapse, pain, and moments so dark they nearly swallowed him whole. But somewhere in that darkness, the Holy Spirit met him, and what happened next is proof that even in the deepest pit, there is a way out.

Here is Jason Rudeen's inspiring story in his words:

'I'm not here to glorify or horrify you with details of my addictions. My story isn't that unique. I never imagined I'd be telling people how I got clean, or how the Holy Spirit radically moved in my life. I thought I was a lifer in the game. I didn't know God at all.

But to understand how I got here, you need to know where I've been.

I grew up in a single-mother household. My parents split before I turned one. As far back as I can remember, my mom, Tammie, drank and smoked weed. I remember the smell, the slurred words. I'm sure there were other substances involved too.

When I was 5, she was in a devastating motorcycle accident. She was launched through the air and suffered extreme injuries, including a traumatic brain injury that left her in a coma for three months. It was considered one of the worst head injuries in Minnesota at the time (in 1985).

While she fought for her life, I went to live with my aunt, uncle, and two cousins. My aunt and uncle worked very long hours. And my cousins were six and sixteen years old. Nikki (6) went to school during the day, and Alan (16) didn't go to a regular school, so he was my babysitter. That's when the unthinkable began. Alan molested me nearly every day for three months. One day, he caught me in the bathroom, and I pushed him with everything I had. He fell into the bathtub. I ran out of the house with no clothes on, through the countryside of Minnesota, pounding on a stranger's door. I told the woman what had happened. She gasped, grabbed me, and called 911.

After that, I went to live with another aunt and uncle. Like many kids, I repressed the trauma for years. Therapy at the time felt more like playtime. I didn't talk much. I didn't even really remember it. But it would all come back.

Eventually, my mom recovered. The version of her I knew post-accident was different from the one before. She won a sizable settlement from the lawsuit and built us a house in Coon Rapids, Minnesota. She was fun most of the time, but she had a temper. She drank a lot in those next few years and met a man. The relationship was volatile. Drinking, parties, and domestic disputes were frequent. I remember dumping her Windsor and flushing her cigarettes, swearing I'd never be like that. Go figure!

The relationship only lasted long enough for them to have two children. By the time I was 8, my brother was born. By age 10, my sister. I practically raised them; I changed diapers, cooking, cleaning, reading stories, while my mom was at work, bars, or friends' houses. Their father was unstable and at times frightening. He'd circle the bars where she hung out and watched our house from his car. I remember always having weapons in case he would try to break in.

At age 12, I started having recurring nightmares: dark, sexually aggressive dreams involving a faceless man and a faceless boy. I became very disturbed and kept it secret for months. I didn't understand what they meant. I wondered if I was the kid . . . or the man. Shame and confusion consumed me. When I finally opened up to my mom, that's when she told me what had happened when I was younger. In that moment, the memories returned, flooding in with painful clarity. It was like a switch flipped and everything I had buried came rushing back.

I tried therapy again. I didn't talk much, but I got really into journaling, music, and writing poetry. I then began to find escape and peace in drugs and alcohol. It became an outlet. My mom was going through her own trouble and started attending AA, though I wouldn't find that out until a year after I was clean. By then, I was carrying deep resentment. And when she tried to step into motherhood again, I rebelled hard.

I cut class. Snuck out. Developed a reputation as a troublemaker and started hanging with the kids who were just as lost and angry as I was. I drank. Smoked weed. Found friends whose parents let us party at their place, their philosophy being it was safer than us being out on the streets. I practically lived there.

From there, I ran away and hopped a train. In the city, I met a man who invited me back to his place. That's when I tried heroin for the first time. I overdosed not long after. At school, I met a girl in choir, my first long-term girlfriend. At fifteen, I was selling weed. By sixteen, I was selling coke, meth, ecstasy, and acid. I picked up the needle again. By seventeen, I was in love, but I had to be high to feel anything. We had a miscarriage the first time she got pregnant. Then she got pregnant again. I was eighteen when my son was born. That same year, I was sexually assaulted by a guy that I thought was my friend while I was passed out drunk. I almost killed the guy later that night. Thankfully I woke up before it went any further. At twenty years old we had our daughter. But the relationship fell apart, and when I was twenty-one, I ran again. Shortly after that, one of my best friends sexually assaulted me when I was asleep after being up for days. I stayed alone for about a year until I met the woman who would become my first wife. Our whole relationship revolved around drugs and the needle.

For the next decade, I spiraled, becoming very self-destructive. I battled addiction, PTSD, anxiety, and depression. It seemed there were no safe spaces in my world. I burned bridges and rebuilt them only to burn them again. I alienated myself from my two children and my first love. I lost jobs; I had so many I can't even count them. I failed at college. Destroyed two marriages. I lost count of how many times I had to start over with nothing. I've lived on the streets. I've walked through hell.

In 2008, I went to treatment to quit shooting up. I was serious about change, but I didn't plug into a healthier community. I didn't surrender. I didn't replace old habits with new ones. I didn't think I was powerless yet, but I knew my life was unmanageable. I ended up having a hard time finding a job, and it wasn't long before I started drinking, smoking weed, and hanging with old friends again. I believed I was doing so good because I wasn't using needles. That was my problem. I was still playing with fire.

Eventually, I met my second wife. We had a son, Wyatt. I was thirty-two, and I hadn't touched hard drugs in four years at this point.

I was so happy, I ended up proposing because I thought it was my second chance to get it right. But my drinking caught up with me. It got out of control and she got sick of my crap, so I got myself kicked out. At thirty-three I was back living with my mom, starting over again. I saw my son on weekends. Got a job in a kitchen. Things were stabilizing, until I relapsed on meth in 2014.

This time, it got dark. Fast. I started selling meth for the cartel through a guy I worked with. I thought I had control. But it was all an illusion. It led me back to the needle and a spiritual death. I lost my visitation rights with my son. My family and friends wrote me off. I was arrested after being set up by a close customer with a large quantity of drugs and was facing one hundred and eleven months in prison. They released me on my own recognizance and staked out my house for months. I wouldn't sell anymore, despite my connection's best efforts to convince me to do so. I was at my bottom, and I couldn't break free from my demons.

At my lowest point, I tried to overdose. Meth-induced psychosis nearly broke me. I attempted to kill myself because I was sure there was no hope for me. I didn't think I'd ever see my son again, just like my two older kids whom I hadn't spoken to in fifteen years at that time.

Through inpatient treatment, outpatient, and three relapses (all after a couple friends died of an overdose), I began to claw my way back. I set up therapy, anger management, parenting classes, and eventually, another inpatient stay. I finally opted for extended care—

four and a half months of it—and started working the steps. For me to get and stay clean, I had to be desperate enough to really want to learn something new.

Now for the good stuff. Recovery. Personal growth. Self-discovery. Forgiveness. Freedom. Grace. Love.

About the first five and a half months of truly working at a program, I felt on fire! I was really digging in. I was following suggestions. I studied hard with others and at home. But I had a secret. I was having a beer at bedtime. Sometimes I wouldn't even finish it. It may sound dumb, but it was an old behavior. It's not enough to learn things in recovery—we have to apply them as well. You know, I can hardly believe I was so trapped in my behavior patterns my whole life. The further I get into recovery, the more it boggles my mind. I was studying my butt off to learn all I could from Narcotics Anonymous (NA), Alcoholic Anonymous (AA), and Crystal Meth Anonymous (CMA). I had a beer most nights while I would study in my bed, highlighting and taking notes. Thinking I was clean because I wasn't catching a buzz.

When I got called on it, I had a decision to make: follow the suggestions and stop the secret beers, or stop the program. It came down to two simple questions for me after a couple of weeks of being pissed off in secret. But first I planned on drinking it up for my birthday weekend. I drank and smoked a bit the night before my actual birthday, and just like they told me, "Nothing is worse than a belly full of booze and a head full of AA." I didn't enjoy it, and I finally asked myself two things:

> Do I want to work the steps and see if they can really change me? Yup.
>
> Do I want to work with Mike? Does he have what I want? Yup!

I finally let go of control and surrendered fully. I told my sponsor, "No more beers, bro!" I'd been so upset because I really didn't think it was a big deal. But when I reset my clean time at all my meetings, the weight lifted off of me said otherwise. I stood at my turning point.

I've come to understand that nothing on this journey of recovery makes sense at first. We have to learn that the right thing is usually uncomfortable to do. I started diving into the Steps. I went through the Recovery Coach Academy at Minnesota Recovery Connection. I did telephone recovery support calls there regularly and even got to be an interviewer for the next round of the Academy.

My sentencing for the drug-dealing charges I'd been arrested for long before this was finally coming up. I asked at some meetings if anyone would be willing to write a letter on my behalf. I had four by the time I went to my court date. When I stood in front of the judge, she came out and began to speak about the moving letters she had received, and there were a lot more than four in her hand. There were thirteen!

She spoke of my service commitments and things people had said in the letters. She finally told me, "Mr. Rudeen, there's no way I'm going to lock you up with all the good you are doing for the community." To this day, I can't get through one of those letters without crying. I'm grateful for those angels in my life. She ended up granting me a downward departure instead of the ninety-eight months in prison. I was floored! The deal came with twenty years of probation, and any violation would send me back to serve the full sentence. I burst into tears. Then, she asked if I'd be willing to speak to high school students in Anoka County. Without hesitation, I said yes!

For almost a year and a half, I was on constant monitoring with a sweat patch. I met every condition of my sentence within nine months. As of September 2023, I was released from probation, and I'm now off all paper. I stay in touch with everyone involved in my case, even the DA! My felony was reduced to a gross misdemeanor once my probation was completed. Miracles!

I found God about a year into my program, and it was completely unexpected. By that point, the principles of the Twelve Steps had already begun to change me. I didn't know at the time that they were biblically based or that they represented universal spiritual truths. I was in extended care at the time, about three and half months into my four-and-half-month stay in the residential program. I was hitting a rough patch. Sundays were visiting days, so the apartments were usually empty; everyone was either at visits or out on a twelve-hour pass. On those Sundays, I'd often find myself in a dark place.

Since friends from CMA and NA would pick up guys for church every week, I decided to join them one Sunday. I didn't want to be alone. I went for the company and the free coffee and donuts, not expecting a spiritual awakening. But the truth is, when you really work the steps and apply the principles of the program to your daily life, it changes you from the inside out. It clears the conduit between you and God. That's how you begin to develop a spiritual life, which is also known as God-consciousness. I had a profound experience of this for over a year before I ever found Christ.

The message that day felt like it was made just for me. It was all about what my relationship with the Lord should look like: one of a child with his father. The pastor's son, who was four years old, helped illustrate the point. He had his son come up on stage, and the little boy just wanted to be picked up. Then, he buried his face in his father's neck, too shy to look up during the message. My own son was also four at the time, and I hadn't seen him in nine months. The pastor talked about the mishaps and failings we experience as parents, and every word hit me deeply. Then he said, "No matter what the need, we should always have our arms wide open, looking to the Father." I was moved!

After nearly three years of attending that church, the pastor did the first—and only—altar call I'd ever seen there. He invited anyone who wanted to ask Jesus into their life to come forward. I felt hesitation right away, but I recognized it as a moment I needed to step through fear, thanks to my recovery. I went up and prayed with him. I remember the band was playing "O Come to the Altar," and the lyrics struck me so deeply that I couldn't stop crying for an hour or more. I looked at my friend, Jim, and said, "What's wrong with me, dude?" He simply placed his hand on my shoulder and said, "That's the Holy Spirit, brother." I believed him, and that feeling hasn't left me since.

This all happened in October 2016, and by Easter Sunday 2017, I was baptized. Additionally, I joined a small group Bible study through my church. Since then, I've trained to be a Stephen Minister, providing one-on-one Christian care. I'm the caregiver; God is the curegiver! For almost four years, I led the baptism team at Grace Fellowship, helping others take this paramount step in their lives. As I continued on my faith journey, my mom began asking a lot of questions about Jesus and wanted to come to church with me. I think she just wanted to see this new aspect of my life. Eventually, she came to faith, and I had the privilege of baptizing her.

A couple of years later, my mom was diagnosed with AML, an aggressive blood cancer. Her battle with leukemia lasted about a year, and she eventually needed a bone marrow transplant. Following the transplant, she required one hundred days of in-home care. I am so grateful that I was in a good place during that time. I was strong in my recovery and was able to work it out with my job to take three and a half months off to stay with my mom, take care of her, and simply spend time together. This was during COVID, so we literally couldn't go anywhere. She had no immune system, so we just hung out, ate a lot of food, watched movies, and talked. It was an amazing time, even though it was scary and hard.

She became cancer free, but that lasted only a few months. When her leukemia came back, none of the treatments that had worked before were effective anymore. My mom ultimately lost her battle with leukemia. This situation brought my brother, sister, and me closer together than ever as we worked to handle her end-of-life matters. And again, something beautiful came out of a hard situation. The peace I felt, knowing her salvation was sealed and she was going home to her Heavenly Father, brought me great comfort during this time. I could see that peace in her too; she was in good spirits right up until her final moments. That was a gift from God, to be sure. This is a blessing I never would have experienced if I hadn't found recovery or God, because I wouldn't have been allowed to be there, nor mentally equipped to handle it. I probably would've gone down the rabbit hole and spiraled out. Blessings indeed!

Today in my life, service work helps me stay clean. Amongst the things I previously mentioned, I also sponsor men and keep in touch with my own sponsor. I am a host of a recovery podcast called "The Way Out Podcast." We have over 450 episodes to date and we aren't stopping. I have made so many friends that are leaders in the recovery advocacy movement. They inspire me, lift me up, and push me to be a better version of myself every day. They give me hope for a brighter future and for the ability to sustain a life in recovery, while being a father to my son and a good brother, uncle, son, friend, partner, and human.

I am certified as a Certified Peer Recovery Specialist (CPRS) and am involved with Mobilize Recovery, Recovery Revolution, The Minnesota Recovery Advocacy Project, and I'm a founding board member of Recovery Cafe Anoka County, which is a peer recovery center in Anoka, MN. My life has a trajectory today. I only need to listen to the Holy Spirit, stay rooted in the Word, and follow His direction for my life. There are always moments of uncomfortability that lead to the best results in my life.

I want to tell you today that anyone can recover. Let someone else who has done it lead the way. Don't let fear stop you from what you deserve. You won't understand it at first, but more will be revealed as you trudge the road of happy destiny. My advice to you would be this: take the leap and surrender! You're worth it!'

Jason's story isn't just about surviving, it's about living free. The man who once thought he was destined to die in his addiction now wakes up each day with purpose, service, and the joy of knowing God's grace is real. His life is proof that no matter how far gone you think you are, there's a road back.

It won't always make sense. It won't always be easy. But as Jason would tell you, the right thing is often the uncomfortable thing. And if you'll take the leap, if you'll surrender, you'll find that the God who met him in his lowest place is the same God who will meet you in yours. Freedom isn't reserved for the few. It's available for anyone willing to reach for it.

CHAPTER 12

Sidewalk Shackles to the Savior: *Corrine's Plot Twist*

The next story I feel called to share is one I came across on YouTube. There's a YouTube creator named Peter Santenello who dares to go where most don't. He films stories for raw and real storytelling. His channel pulls back the curtain on the stories that matter, the ones we rarely see on the evening news. While writing this book, I came across one of his episodes, and it felt like a divine interruption. You know the kind, when God gently taps your shoulder and says, *"Pay attention."*

The episode was titled *Inside America's #1 Epidemic*[1]. It followed a ride-along with two outreach workers from the Phoenix Rescue Mission in Arizona: Corrine and a gentleman partner. But it was Corrine's story that branded itself on my heart.

They were out doing street outreach, driving into tent cities, approaching people camped out in alleys, behind shopping centers, and under overpasses. They handed out hygiene kits, bottled water, and most importantly, dignity. But what Corrine said hit the hardest. She told Peter in their interview that they have services available for the homeless. They have housing and programs. But she pointed out that they would have to want the help. That's the real battle.

That truth got me thinking. So often we assume homelessness is about a lack of shelter, or addiction is about a lack of discipline, or brokenness is about a lack of effort. But really it's not about the "worldly" things. Corrine saw something deeper. She'd lived it.

She went on to explain that she had been homeless, addicted to fentanyl, and living in the streets off and on for five years. She discussed how she had been in and out of rehab. In and out of services. On Subutex for three and a half years.

Then she proceeded to say that something was missing. She said, "I don't know how to explain it, but it was Jesus."

That sentence hit me with the kind of force that only truth can carry. The truth that transformation isn't just about behavior change, it's about the heart. The soul. The *why* beneath the pain. Corrine said, "You wouldn't recognize me two and a half years ago." Peter stood in awe as he watched her fearlessly approach people others hesitate to go near. But Corrine wasn't seeing addicts. She was seeing *people*.

She said, "The drugs are part of a bigger issue," but they are just people like you and me, and I knew exactly what she meant. Because I've said it too.

There's something sacred about seeing someone beyond their circumstances. Something I've carried with me into prisons, recovery groups, and those I worked with on the streets. I see the *person*. Not the prison. Not the pain. And when people feel seen, really seen, that can create an opening to the doorway for change. Not out of guilt. Not out of obligation. But because something inside of them begins to stir. *Hope awakens when love sees us.*

Corrine's story is a testimony to that kind of hope. She didn't get clean from medication or the various help and services she partook in. She didn't get off the streets just because someone handed her a housing voucher. She got clean and set free because she encountered the One who makes all things new. The only One who could reach the parts of her soul that drugs numbed but never healed. Jesus. And now, here she is; walking the same streets, but not as a prisoner. As a *rescuer*.

Corrine's plot twist continues to highlight the message of this entire book: Not every prison has bars. Some are made of cardboard, syringes, and shame. But Jesus walks through all of them. He is not afraid of the mess. He doesn't flinch at the scars. He came for the sick, the addicted, the forgotten. He came for all of us no matter our circumstance.

We don't just need better systems. We need soul healing. Because if the soul isn't free, the body will find a way to stay caged. Even when the door is open. Corrine is living proof that even in the grip of addiction, even after years on the pavement, even in the darkest cycle, Jesus was the missing piece to lasting recovery. And when you find Him—or rather, open your heart to Him—He's there, waiting with open arms. When we connect with our Being (Spirit), that's when everything changes, and chains that once felt unbreakable begin to fall.[124]

Footnote:

[1]Peter Santenello, *Inside America's #1 Epidemic*, YouTube, January 10, 2024, https://www.youtube.com/watch?v=YFUnQlR-RcI

CHAPTER 13

The Truth That Couldn't Be Burned: Karissa's Plot Twist

Before we dive into Karissa's story, I want to pause for a moment and widen the lens. So far, the stories in this book have walked us through prisons shaped by addiction, homelessness, and incarceration. But those are just the surface layers. If you trace them back far enough, you'll find a common thread: unseen wounds that began in the heart and mind long before the external circumstances ever took hold.

Addiction, for example, is a byproduct—a symptom of deeper pain. Jason Smith's journey into years of addiction and prison began with the absence of love and the ache of fatherlessness with the lie that he wasn't worth staying for. Jason Rudeen's story echoed the same tune: childhood trauma, planted seeds of unworthiness, and those lies grew until they became chains. Both men were imprisoned by what they believed about themselves long before drugs, prison walls, and bottles ever appeared.

Because that's where prisons begin: not outside of us, but inside our own minds. Lies whispered in pain, accepted as truth. False identities formed in the aftermath of trauma. These lies fester in silence, creating strongholds that eventually manifest in outward bondage: addiction, violence, homelessness, depression.

Karissa's story invites us into a different kind of prison, a more subtle, but no less painful prison. The prison of religious performance and spiritual confusion. Her bondage wasn't addiction or homelessness. It was the invisible pressure to *earn* God's love. To measure up. To silence doubt. To belong to a belief system that left little room for questions or personal truth.

She experienced obedience laced with fear, identity fused with institution, and a version of God that felt more conditional than comforting. This is a story of unraveling. Of stripping everything away—beliefs, roles, spiritual scaffolding—and standing face to face with the raw unknown. What Karissa found on the other side wasn't rebellion. It wasn't new-age enlightenment or anti-faith cynicism.

What she found was Christ.

But not the Christ confined to a church. What she found was the living, radiant frequency of Christ Himself; truth that could not be counterfeited. Light that could not be distorted. Love that could not be earned. And in finding Him, she found herself.

Before I share her story, it is important to acknowledge this: Christ Himself is not confined to a building, an institution, or a denomination. He is the living, breathing Son of God, the embodiment of love and truth, and He meets us in the wilderness just as much as He meets us in the sanctuary. While I have recently come to personally stand on the truth of the Bible and find deep wisdom in the words of Jesus recorded there, I also believe this: Christ is for everyone. He is not owned by any church. He is not limited by human structures. His love flows beyond borders, beyond the walls we build, and beyond the systems that sometimes distort His image.

This book is written through the lens of the Christian faith, a faith in which I've found both truth and freedom, even as I continue to wrestle with aspects of it. But I want to gently remind you again in plain words: **Christ is not a religion.** Christ is the living presence of God's love— personal, relational, and deeply pursuing. He is the One who meets us in our humanity, not with rules, but with restoration. A relationship with Christ is as unique and personal as the person who holds it. Some encounter Him in the pews of a church. Others find Him in a moment of surrender—alone in their car, in the quiet of nature, or in the breaking open of their soul. He meets us where we are and speaks in the language our hearts can understand. I know this because He has spoken to me in many ways, through many different means, throughout my journey of growing closer to Him.

At the same time, one of the most important things I've come to learn is that Scripture calls us to discernment, because not everything that *feels* spiritual is from God. The Bible warns us that "Satan himself masquerades as an angel of light" (2 Corinthians 11:14). There is a very real enemy who seeks to twist, mimic, and counterfeit the things of God. I wrestled with this for a long time. But I'm coming to understand that while the spirit realm is absolutely real, so is spiritual warfare. That's why we're instructed to test every spirit (1 John 4:1) and to hold every revelation, message, or experience up to the light of Christ.

Karissa's story is a breathtaking testimony of this. An awakening to her spiritual gifts as a medium while simultaneously discovering Christ outside the confines of religion and using Him as her guide. Her journey is raw, courageous, and deeply resonant with the truth that Jesus can meet us in unexpected places. While every faith journey is personal and often complex, I believe her story points us back to the same unshakable truth: **Christ is not bound by human traditions.** He is the light that cannot be counterfeited, the love that cannot be earned, and the presence that will find you, no matter where you stand.

I am deeply honored to share Karissa's story in her words:

"Leaving wasn't a moment. It was years of a thousand tiny deaths. We didn't slam a door and walk out in defiance. It was more like watching your own house burn down, knowing it's the only place you've ever lived and still striking the match yourself. There's no words for the way it unravels you, and it doesn't happen from one day to the next. It is often years of what you thought you knew, what you're learning now, and how you feel completely at war with each of those every single day. It's to live with an inner battle that the people around you would never know you are fighting.

I was a devout Mormon, born from a lineage deeply rooted in the faith. My husband was the same. It was in our blood, in our bones. When we married, we raised our four children without question, faithfully adhering to the traditions that had shaped us. For almost forty years, I poured my whole heart into the system that raised me— until my body broke down, my spirit cracked open, and the scaffolding of religion could no longer hold the weight of my truth. I began to see the cost of a belief system steeped in guilt, shame, and unworthiness; where blessings were conditional and God's love was earned through strict obedience.

Choosing to leave is so much more than a quiet exit and a change of course. It's so hard to put into words how it feels, because how do you explain walking away from the only world you've ever known? How do you explain that your entire sense of self was fused to a belief system? How do you explain that your worth was measured by obedience and performance? That your community was contingent? That your thoughts, your feelings, even your body, were never fully yours? How do you explain that leaving felt like liberation and death at the same time?

You don't just leave Mormonism. You leave an identity you didn't know you had.

I didn't choose the beliefs initially, I was born into them. They were sung into me at bedtime, spoken at the dinner table, stitched into every holiday, every choice, every relationship. They were woven into every thread of my life. They were second nature. They were safety, security, and comfort all at the same time. And when I became a mother, I became the one singing at bedtime, stitching the same beliefs into my children. It was never *just* church.

But the cracks grew too loud, and we couldn't unsee what we had seen. Which meant when I left, I didn't just lose a Sunday schedule, I lost a spiritual ecosystem. Family ties shifted. Friendships evaporated. My name changed on people's lips.

And the grief? It starts long before you exit. It begins in the ache you carry in silence, when you feel the internal conflict but you still show up. When your mouth sings hymns your heart no longer feels. When you sit in church and force a smile while something inside you has already withered. By the time I finally spoke the truth out loud, that we were done, I had already grieved it all. The day we left was not the rupture. It was the release.

I had to learn how to trust my own voice. To feel the difference between peace and programming. Between a real "yes" and a conditioned "yes." Between discernment and the fear of being wrong.

And I grieved God. I didn't know what was real. I was untangling my identity from my indoctrination. Did any of my divine experiences prior to that actually happen or were they fabricated out of my own imagination? My own wanting them to be true? I couldn't trust them now. I couldn't tell where Jesus ended and the programming began.

So I let it all burn.

My spiritual gifts expanded exponentially after I left the church. I realized I was a medium, a bridge between the physical and spiritual world. When I look back over the course of my life, I can see how this gift had been there all along. It wasn't new. It was buried beneath layers of belief that had kept me from recognizing what had always been right in front of me.

Once those layers fell away, the spirit world opened like floodgates. I began receiving visitations in my waking and sleeping hours. The messages that came through were so specific, so beautiful, so layered with love that I couldn't deny what was happening. Classmates' cousins. Friends-of-friends' children. People I'd either just met or hadn't spoken to in years. If I had even a thread of connection to someone on this side, the other side showed up.

I didn't want to turn it off, but I didn't know how to manage it all either. I didn't know if, or how, to share such profound and sometimes painfully tender messages. I was getting nothing done in my waking life and I didn't really know how to reconcile everything I was experiencing. All I could do was chalk it up to something "divine."

I reached out to a trusted, non-religious friend and told her plainly: "I think I'm a medium."

She didn't flinch. "Of course you are," she said. She was too.

I asked her thoughts about protection, light, and working between worlds. She paused. "Do you want the new age answer or the real one?"

I said, "Give me the real one."

Her reply: "You need to use Christ in everything you do."

I was shocked. I had spent the last year throwing everything out that even smelled like religion. And there it was again: Christ. I tossed it over my shoulder. Not interested. Not that name. Not that story. Not that system.

In the two and a half years spent working between worlds since then, I've learned some hard lessons and really important truths that shifted everything for me. Spiritual gifts are powerful. But without discernment, it is very easy to be misguided.

As I stripped everything away and rebuilt my spiritual life from the inside out, I was stunned to find Christ at the center. It was a revelation that pulled the rug out from under me all over again! Christ came back. Not in a sermon. Not in a scripture. Not in a building.

The Christ I found was a living frequency of love and truth that had been there all along, waiting to be remembered. It took some time for me to even be open to that, which is the prerequisite. A softening into our places that will not yield. Because Christ's presence won't come by force, it comes by allowance or invitation. Which isn't always saying, "Christ, come into my life." It can also be how it was for me: *"I'm willing to be shown what I don't know."*

I didn't know that light can be mimicked, counterfeited, and distorted. I didn't realize that deception is everywhere, even in the spirit world. I didn't think it was true, because I didn't want it to be true. It's beautiful to connect with the other side. To hold messages for loved ones. To offer higher timelines and healing. But if we believe we don't need protection, if we think we can navigate the spirit world without discernment . . . we are deeply mistaken. Light without truth we can trust is not light at all.

The universal Law of Polarity teaches that everything has two poles—opposites that are actually different expressions of the same essence. Light and dark, hot and cold, love and fear, expansion and contraction. They're not separate—they exist on the same spectrum. You can't truly understand one without encountering the other. This law shows us that contrast is necessary for clarity. You understand peace by knowing chaos. You recognize truth because you've encountered distortion. Every experience holds its counterpart.

In spiritual work, the Law of Polarity reminds us that just because something is spiritual doesn't mean it's benevolent. Not all light is true light. Not all voices whisper love. This is why discernment is essential—we must learn to feel into the frequency, not just trust the form.

Christ has become the measure I hold everything up to. Now, in every reading, every channeling, every offering, I begin by connecting to the light of Christ. Because it is the *only* light I trust. The only light that cannot be counterfeited. The only frequency that burns through deception and reveals only what is true. The Christ Light is more than the cleanest light I know; it is the cleanest light there *is*.

Christ is not the center of any denomination, He is the code of truth woven through all things, the code and the keeper. Jesus was the code. He embodied the pattern. The living demonstration. He carried the divine blueprint of unconditional love, radical truth, resurrection, forgiveness, presence. Christ is the keeper. Christ is the eternal consciousness that holds, transmits, and activates the code across time and dimension. Christ isn't limited to Jesus—it's the living field that holds that frequency for all of us to access now.

One walked the earth. The other lives forever outside the boundary of form. Jesus carried the code. Christ is the current of frequency that keeps it alive.

In a vision I had once, I was taken to the chapel within the only church I'd known for almost forty years. I walked past each row, my hand gently touching the backrest of each pew. The sacrament table draped with a white lace covering, the podium & microphone, the grand piano and organ pipes. The white walls and high ceilings. It was all there. It felt warm and familiar. There was a comfort. I felt settling and safety in my body. Safety—*oh yes*. It always comes back to that. I took notice that there were no people in this image, and that made me realize something: the comfort and safety I felt was not in the people, it was in the structure!

The structure was the container! It made this big unknown world small, simple, and easier to manage. I didn't miss the people, the talks, the lessons or practices. I was longing for a container of safety. The chapel was somewhere I could go, something I could count on. It wasn't the building itself, it's what the building provided.

I held a quiet fear of exploring too far beyond the parameters that I once knew. What was out there? With no borders or limits, what would I find? And then I saw the Crystalline grid and realized, *oh yes*! Universal Structure! It's bigger and more vast but it's still there! There's still a container! Everything is held: everything is known and watched. Ah, *safety*. I can trust this. Structure provided the safety my system was yearning for. And Christ is the truth held within each frame of this grid because he *is* the framework. Christ *is* the safety.

Many of my experiences with God and Christ I picked back up because I realized they didn't belong to the system, they belonged to the Source. The Christ I know moves through dimensions. Never pushy, never insistent, whose presence alone *is* the power.

I left religion but reclaimed my spirituality in a very intimate, personal way. Our true nature is spirit, and no matter how much we resist it, some part of us will always long to return to this place of knowing; to experience the divine and our relationship with it. And we will be restless until we do. Spirituality for me has changed shape over the years. But even in the uncertainty, deposits of trust were continually made. Whether I knew what I believed, or if I believed at all, I was surprised to find that some truths can't be burned. They only reveal themselves once the fire passes. God and Christ were still there, beyond the border of *all* religions, patiently waiting for my return.

The second coming is a return to what we once knew, that Christ *is*. He *is* universal law, divine order, pure truth, and the direct path to the one and only Source of All: God. Christ is a divine authority that is recognized by every force in this Universe, and I don't have to understand it all to know that it's true. I've lived it. I've tried with and without. I did not expect it, but I fully accept it.

God meets us where we are, in the language we'll understand, because that's what love does. And for me, for a time, that was in the system of religion. But to echo the words of Marianne Williamson, I've come to know for myself that Christ belongs to no one—and to everyone. No institution has ownership of universal truth.

I am born again. Made new in this knowing that cleanses all doubt, fear, and confusion. Today, my records are nowhere. In no archives of any religious institutional system and yet . . . my name is imprinted in the palms of my Savior. And the name of Christ is etched deeply within every layer of my heart."

Karissa's journey is a powerful one, discovering the truth that cannot be burned: Christ is at the center of everything. Her story points to a peace that can only be found in Him. It isn't about rejecting faith, but about returning to its source. In leaving religion, she found Christ, the Christ who is not bound to pews or programs, but who moves freely through every dimension, every heart, and every moment of surrender. And that's the invitation her story leaves us with: to let go of our expectations of what we think God has to look like, and to open our hearts to the One who already knows us, loves us, and calls us by name. In that place, we discover the freedom our souls have been searching for, in the language only our souls can understand.

CHAPTER 14

The Real Wealth: Lindsay's Plot Twist

This chapter has been the hardest to write. Maybe because, even as I type these words, I'm still in the thick of it. Still in the middle of my mess. Still staring at the wreckage of years of financial dysfunction and trying to make sense of it all while learning to walk in peace anyway. The truth is, I feel waves of guilt and shame wash over me. Not because I don't believe in grace—oh, I do. But because the weight of my decisions have impacted not just me, but my family too.

But if there's anything I've been learning, it's this: freedom doesn't always come when the mess is over. Sometimes it comes right in the middle of it. God keeps bringing me back to surrender. Back to trust. Back to His feet, where I find a peace I shouldn't have in the middle of a reality like this one.

So this is my *Plot Twist*. Not the kind where everything magically resolves and we live happily ever after. But the kind where, even while

I'm still standing in the rubble, I can look you in the eye and say: I'm free. Even here.

For most of my life, money has been both a mystery and a mirage. I started working at eleven years old, babysitting and spending every dollar I earned. Saving wasn't in my vocabulary. Budgeting? Never learned it. We didn't talk about money in my house. I grew up in a middle to upper-class family where needs were always met, and most wants were too. Not that I had everything handed to me, but I didn't really have much of a concept of what it meant to go without.

That early relationship with money set a pattern I never grew out of. I became a giver, a spender, and someone who always lived beyond her means. And while generosity is beautiful, undisciplined generosity paired with poor money management is a recipe for disaster. Add in a credit card or five, and I was deep in a cycle of debt with no roadmap out.

My husband and I both brought financial wounds into our marriage. He was self-employed and had developed a pattern of not paying taxes due to overspending with his ex-wife. Then, it continued with us. Years ago, when we sold our home in Colorado to move to Arizona, the IRS took every bit of our equity. After that, we were deemed "uncollectible" and tried to stay on track. But the patterns didn't change.

We rented for seven years in Arizona—no savings, mounting debt, barely staying ahead of the minimum payments. Then two years ago, I unfortunately lost my wedding ring. It had been custom designed by my husband. Thankfully, it was insured, and we received a $16,000 reimbursement.

I told my husband I wanted to put it toward a house instead of a ring. I had the best of intentions that felt like a better investment. But that meant we had to scrape together everything we could and in doing so, between the down payment, the high interest rate, and no change in spending habits, we fell behind on taxes again.

Now here we are. Hundreds of thousands in back taxes . . . again. Drowning in debt. Credit cards maxed. No savings. Late on bills. Calls from collectors. And the very real possibility of potentially needing to sell our home. From the outside, though, none of this shows. And that's the part I need to say out loud: what looks picture-perfect on the outside is often just that—a picture. A filtered frame. A curated moment.

While writing this chapter, a friend I met through work reached out and asked to meet. She had been following my journey; she saw me publish a book, launch a podcast, start a clothing brand, go to an island, write a second book, return to the island, film a TV show, and share all these things that look so beautiful and inspiring. And they are. But she sat across from me on our zoom chat and said, "Honestly, I was feeling a little envy. I've been praying about it, and God told me, "Go lift her." So here I am . . . how can I support you?"

That moment cracked something open in both of us. She finally saw the real story behind the highlight reel—the truth beneath the assumptions we compare ourselves to, the ones that leave us feeling envious or inadequate over a reality that doesn't even exist. And in that moment, I felt God speak so clearly: *"Share your journey openly and authentically as you walk through this financial mess. Don't just show the victories. Show the valley. Show the whole story."* So here I am. Showing it.

Back in November 2024, I knew a transition was coming. My job, which had sustained us, was also costing me the one thing I was no longer willing to sacrifice: time with my family. Earning six figures was great, but not at the expense of the people who matter most. I can't leave this life with a bank account full and a soul bankrupt. It became crystal clear that, in the end, the only things that will matter to me are God and my family, so it was time to put them first.

We were already barely staying afloat. Still, I prayed: "God, what do I do with my job?" His answer was not what I expected: "Just wait." Not the answer I wanted, but I realized it was an invitation to continue to practice surrender. So I waited. After the new year, I attended a JOA authors' event, and Keira, the founder, shared about her yearlong Mosai Masters program: business mentorship, a private island retreat to write and publish a book, a TV show called *Writer's Island*, and more. As she spoke, I knew in my spirit it was a "holy hell yes." Then she shared the price—$77,000—and I laughed to myself. That was a "holy hell no".

Still, I decided at that moment to say a quiet prayer, "God, if this is meant to be, make it happen." The event ended. I walked out to my car, pulled away from the venue, and my phone rang. It was a fellow

JOA author I was just beginning to get to know. We had met briefly at her book launch several months earlier, and then we podcasted together earlier that day. She lost her husband to suicide, and our missions felt deeply aligned.

She said, "Lindsay, I'm driving home, and God is speaking loud and clear to me. I'm supposed to help you get into Mosai Masters." She paused, then continued, "At first, I thought maybe I'd help fundraise or donate. But then I heard: 'Pay her way.' I asked God three times, and the answer didn't change. "I'm supposed to pay your full way." Shock overcame me. I was stunned. Completely speechless.

My very first thought was, *"I can't accept that."* That level of generosity felt hard to receive, especially from someone I was just getting to know. But then I heard God whisper, "You said if it was meant to be, make it happen." And here it was. Just an hour after my simple prayer, God was speaking to this woman, and she wasn't just hearing the call, she was obeying it. It was a moment where I deeply felt the beauty of surrender and obedience on both our parts. A miracle unfolding in real time.

I gathered myself and said, "I don't know what to say. Thank you doesn't feel like enough." She replied, "It's enough. It's all God." And she was right. I shared with her the simple prayer I had whispered just an hour earlier—and now, here was God, answering it in a way that left me completely undone. I was blown away by His timing, His provision, and the way He used her generosity and obedience to speak directly to my heart. In that moment, I didn't just feel seen, I felt the weight of the calling He has on my life. A holy reminder that He's not just walking beside me . . . He's leading me. And if I keep choosing surrender and obedience, He will always take me where I'm meant to go.

That moment, and so many others like it, have taught me to trust His voice, even when I can't see the next step. So when February came, I prayed again: "God, what do I do with my job?" And this time, the answer was clear. June 1st would be my last day. I obeyed. And just like I knew it would, the financial bottom dropped out.

We had to stop paying our credit cards. At one point we fell behind on our mortgage and car payments. The back taxes are lingering. Bankruptcy is on the table. So here we are stuck in the messy middle, buried under the rubble. And yet, in Him I have a sense of peace in the middle of the chaos. I feel clarity I've never felt before. I see God's hand gently stripping us down so we can finally rebuild on a new foundation: His foundation.

Give first. Save second. Live on the rest. God is teaching me what I was never taught. And He's using rock bottom to do it. As I was writing this book, a sweet friend invited several of us authors to her luxurious mountain home in Park City, Utah. It was breathtaking, like stepping into a painting. As I sat in stillness overlooking the mountains, I whispered, "God . . . I have nothing. And yet I'm surrounded by abundance."

And He whispered back, "That's the point. I'm teaching you to be content in lack. To see wealth not in dollars, but in people. In faith. In family. In my presence." And then that reality came flooding back that when it's all said and done, when I'm on my deathbed, I won't care about my bank account. The material things. My career. My success. All that matters is Him and the people I love.

I know now, more than ever before after losing my son, that I will never again put work before my family. No job. No paycheck. No opportunity will be worth sacrificing the people I love most. I would rather have nothing and be with my family than have everything and miss their lives.

When I look around at my husband beside me, and my three beautiful kids who are still here with me, I realize: I am rich. Because the only thing I am guaranteed for the rest of my life is a relationship with God, so that comes first. And having my family? That is a complete blessing. Every single day I get with them is wealth beyond measure. It's the REAL wealth.

And that's the plot twist I didn't see coming: I will be okay. I'm not bound by this circumstance. I didn't find freedom when the chaos ended. I found it here, right in the middle of the mess. Right where God meets me, every time. Because true freedom doesn't come when life is perfect—that will never be the case for anyone. It begins when we let God do the deep work inside us. When we surrender our pride, our plans, and our false sense of control, and let Him transform our hearts from the inside out, leading our steps to places far greater than we could ever lead ourselves. I've come to know this, not just in theory, but in the living proof of my own story and through the witnessing of others' stories.

Freedom comes not when the storm clears, but when peace enters the storm. Not when we gain more, but when we need less. Not when everything is fixed around us, but when everything is real within us. This is where the chains start to fall. Right here.

In the surrender.

In the stillness.

In the sacred unraveling that leads us home to Him.

And that . . . that, my friend, is where true freedom begins.

CHAPTER 15

Healing Against All Odds: Brooke's Plot Twist

We will wrap up our testimonies of freedom found through the one who can break all chains no matter the circumstances we face with Brooke's testimony. Brooke's story is one of both darkness and light; one of unimaginable suffering that ultimately led to profound healing. As you read her testimony, you will understand the power of resilience, the impact of hope, and the miraculous ways that God steps in to offer His grace and deliverance. This chapter, like so many others in *Plot Twist*, exemplifies the journey from life's darkest prisons, whether mental, emotional, circumstantial or physical, to a place of redemption and freedom.

Brooke's battle with both postpartum psychosis and chronic illness took her to the very edge of despair. She questioned her faith, wondered daily if she could survive, and struggled deeply in the silence of her pain. Yet, God was never absent. He intervened in ways she couldn't have foreseen and led her to a place of healing, where she found the strength to share her story and help others who walk in similar shadows. Her journey is a testament to the power of persistence, prayer, and the unwavering belief that God's plan is always greater than our own.

Though filled with unimaginable pain, Brooke's journey is ultimately one of redemption and light. Her story will remind you that healing is always possible, even from the most oppressive of prisons, and that God's love never fails, even when we are at our lowest.

I am grateful I get to share Brooke's Story with you all in her words:

'I have the unique experience of enduring postpartum psychosis for eighteen months, followed immediately by a chronic illness journey. Years of seemingly separate medical symptoms all came to a head, and my life, one that had just been getting back on track, seemed to implode. Now healed from both mental and physical illness, I spend my days sharing my story with those still wandering in the darkness. When I was struggling, I didn't have stories of other survivors to light my pathway. I wandered in that darkness for far too long, completely hopeless.

Stuck in the loop of my mind, I wondered why God would ever allow me to suffer as I had. I am fairly certain I'll never know the answer to that question, but I do know this: I have the opportunity and the faith to share my story boldly, with Jesus at the center of it. As long as I am asked to share, my answer will always be yes, because God has worked numerous miracles in my life. The first one being that I am still here today, despite all odds, despite the statistics.

It all began when I was ten days postpartum with my fourth son. I was rocking side to side after tucking my other three toddlers into bed. The first week postpartum went seemingly smoothly, but I could feel the anxiety rising, waiting for the other shoe to drop. That night, the shoe dropped. It was the first hallucination of my postpartum psychosis journey. Terrified, I stopped moving. Just standing there, holding my newborn, I stared at the TV, pretending nothing had happened, wondering if my husband would confirm what I had just experienced. But he didn't. He watched the show, oblivious to the war happening inside my head. I couldn't be sure it hadn't happened, but I also couldn't explain it.

The days became slower, the nights longer. The sleepless nights of caring for a new baby were hard enough without adding a mental health battle. I wasn't a stranger to postpartum depression and anxiety, but this was different. I knew something was seriously wrong.

I begged God to spare me from whatever I was experiencing. I knew He could just take it, so why wouldn't He? I'm not sure when my husband began to notice I was struggling, but always being fairly in tune with each other, I'm sure the daily tears were not the first clue I wasn't myself. We both deep down were probably hoping whatever it was would pass on its own.

Around two months postpartum was the first time I intended to take my life.

But God . . .

God always intervened. Every time. He used my mother's heart, He used timing, He used the illness of our family photographer, and He used my selfish human heart to keep me fighting. I couldn't imagine my husband remarrying or loving another person, so I put the gun down and screamed in my closet, cursing God for not allowing me to go through with it. I threw things in my closet in a fit of rage, and my baby, safely buckled in his swing, would scream like he had fallen out, so I had to go check on him.

Over and over, God intervened like this for months. Before I knew it, my baby was six months old, and Christmas, along with one of my kids' birthdays, was around the corner. I decided I couldn't be the mom who ruined Christmas forever for my kids, so I endured with a fake smile and a prayer. Afterward, I finally opened up to my husband, admitting I was fighting suicidal thoughts. I didn't tell him I suspected postpartum psychosis, but I did say I needed to wean the baby and get him to take a bottle so that my food options would open up. Maybe that, along with getting rid of the breastfeeding hormones, would be enough to make it stop.

My husband was incredibly supportive, willing to do anything he could to help me. Additionally, we were at a transition with his career. We had been trying to sell our house to decrease monthly expenses so my husband could focus more on real estate. After some discussion, we decided to take the leap. He would leave his job before our house had sold to pursue real estate full-time. That decision brought me hope, the kind I needed to keep going. My husband would be home more; I wouldn't be nursing any longer; maybe nobody would need to know how dark these months had been for me. Maybe, just maybe, it could be the skeleton in my closet I would take to my grave.

Turns out, that wouldn't be the case, and had I known I would wrestle the devil for another year before getting hospitalized, I don't think I would have made it.

But God.

He knew. He gave me just enough hope each time I needed it to keep going, to put one foot in front of the other.

By the time my baby's first birthday came, I was managing but still struggling. I was paranoid and convinced that my kids deserved someone better. I didn't know how I would get through another winter. So, I did the only thing I could think of. I wrote my husband a two-page letter, confessing everything: my suicide attempt, my thoughts of postpartum psychosis, and my deep hatred for life. I could no longer carry this alone.

In all honesty, I wished I had opened up fully to my husband a year prior. The next few weeks were filled with hard honest conversations, very little sleep, and many calls to medical professionals leaving voicemails for help and guidance. We were met with very minimal responses. Eventually, help arrived in the form of a family doctor and a new therapist, all working together with my husband to save my life.

I will pass over the ugly painful details of these weeks. The darkness I fought doesn't need further explanation for anyone who has been there. The words just don't exist to fully explain that level of suffering to someone who doesn't battle mental illness. But if I could tell myself anything in those moments, it would be: Just keep going. My life was worth fighting for. And so is yours.

And God wasn't done with me, though I couldn't believe it at the time. It's even hard to comprehend now. I was hospitalized in January of 2019, began medication to treat my postpartum psychosis, and was released five days later as a numb zombie back to my husband's care. The hospital was hard and painful, leaving me with new wounds. I believe there is a common misconception that the mental hospital fixes you. Reality is, it just patches you enough to send you back into the world where the real work must begin with your new, or maybe not new, team of medical professionals. From there, I would spend many months attending weekly therapy with my husband, working with a psychiatrist every four-six weeks in the beginning and still keeping tabs with my primary care doctor.

God showed up for me in countless ways during those two years, and there were many times when He felt silent. It was in both His silence and His presence that I have grown to have the faith I now have in Him. I have been carried through the unimaginable and this part of the story was just the beginning.

Just before my son's second birthday, I found myself crying in bed one night, not because I was upset, but because the cloud that had been following me for two years was finally gone. It passed like the flick of a light switch, and I knew at that moment, it was a miracle. It wasn't the right combination of medications or therapy that did it, it was God. It was too unexplainable to be anything but Him.

We celebrated my son's second birthday with more zeal that year because we were so grateful that I was alive. My wedding anniversary was just after that, so my husband and I went on a weekend getaway to find our marriage again. To shift out of caregiver and back into husband and wife. What a wonderful weekend it was. Full of hope, daydreaming, gratitude, and even joy. Emotions I had feared I would never feel again.

But the bliss was short-lived. I could not have predicted what would happen next. I've come to understand this is why we don't know our futures. Six weeks after my anniversary getaway, I found myself in complete paralysis, staring at a hospital ceiling with my husband in the chair next to me. My ability to speak was inconsistent. I sounded like a robot malfunctioning at best when I could gather words. After multiple tests, scans, and bloodwork, the neurosurgeon walked into my room and declared it was my postpartum depression returning. We laughed. It was so outrageous to us that this would be the doctor's analysis of my condition. I had just seen my own psychiatrist and was informed I scored extremely well on the happiness test they had me take each visit. Higher than the average American, which this neurologist couldn't care less about. He wanted me to see his psychiatrist, go back to inpatient and work with an occupational therapist until I could walk again.

This was a quick HELL NO. Once again, my amazing husband stood by me and said, "You'll discharge her now, or I'll sign an AMA (against medical advice) and take her home." I have never been discharged so fast from a hospital.

This was the beginning of my physical illness journey. You can read more about the details of this journey in my book, *Through Fire and Grace*. For here I will say I have no doubt in God's timing. It has not been easy, but I have seen God's fingerprints all over it.

In that short window between my mental and physical illness journey, I had gotten my first tattoo on my forearm. Written like a cross, it says "faith", to serve as a daily reminder that it was God alone who brought me through wrestling with the devil for two years. As I sat in the hospital in paralysis, I looked down at my arm and was overwhelmed with peace in the complete unknown. I knew if God had taken me through the hell I just walked, He would be with me through anything.

I took each day as it came. Never looking too far ahead. Never wondering how many years this illness would take my life and finding contentment in living in the present. The months of therapy I had done and was still attending helped me process my diagnosis and kept me in a good head space.

Through it all, God was in the details of my journey. I discovered that I had skull and neck instability, the root cause being a genetic disorder, compounded by injuries I had sustained when I was younger. We learned that only five surgeons in the world were skilled enough to perform my surgery, but the two in America declined my case. In the end, this turned out to be a blessing in disguise.

The surgeon I had hoped to see was located in Barcelona, Spain. Although it wasn't practical to fly halfway across the world to see a specific doctor, I reached out to him after the American doctors declined my case. I filled out the extensive questionnaires once again and had to travel for the imaging he requested, as there were no upright MRI machines in Utah at the time.

On New Year's Eve 2019, I felt a nudge to check my spam email. I had saved the surgeon's email but didn't expect anything to be there. To my surprise, just a few emails down, I found the long-awaited message from him. He confirmed everything I had suspected through my research, diagnosing my instability and confirming conditions like Chiari malformation, Myalgic Encephalomyelitis/Chronic Fatigue Syndrome (ME/CFS), Mast Cell Activation Syndrome (MCAS), and Hypermobile Ehlers-Danlos Syndrome (HEDS), to name a few.

It was such a validating feeling to be told by a specialist that I was a classic case, completely textbook to him, after spending my life being told my symptoms didn't add up. To finally have a doctor name and understand my condition and believe that he could help gave me a sense of overwhelming gratitude. I could hardly believe it.

After a video appointment with my newfound hope, I waited patiently for the email with the price to come through. Two days later, I opened the email and saw the cost. It was going to take a miracle to afford it. Without missing a beat, my husband said, "We'll just sell our house to pay for it." In no time, our home was on the market, and we were back in the waiting game. We held open houses, scheduled appointments, and the clock was ticking. We had to pay for the surgery in full before traveling to Barcelona. Although my appointment was still a few months away, the waiting was excruciating. Living each day in constant pain, I wore a hard neck brace and walked with two forearm crutches, feeling like my head was about to explode 24/7. I parented my four young children from the floor, the couch, or even bed, just trying to be as present with them as I could in such unbearable pain.

The weeks passed and our house had not sold. It was the tail end of winter in Utah, which is not the best time to be selling. Then, in the 11th hour, God came through. A family offered full price on our home and put a closing date that would allow us to receive the funds the day before we would need to wire the money to the hospital. Everything was lining up perfectly. Thank you, Jesus!

If you're following the timeline, you may have noticed this would put us right in the middle of March, 2020. Yes, the year Covid hit the world, shut us down for "two weeks" and changed everything. The weekend we moved out of our home, the schools shut down for "two weeks", stores started requiring masks, and the world seemed unpredictable.

As for my life-saving surgery, I thought 'everything had lined up too perfectly for this to not go through. God wouldn't do that to me . .

. could you imagine that chapter in my book, the one where my surgery was canceled? Yeah, me neither. '

Yet, when I was just a week from flying out to Barcelona for my surgery, I got a call. Not a good sign, as the doctor's office had never called me before. I answered, and as you may be sensing at this point, I got the devastating news that my surgery was being postponed until the hospital was allowed to open again. They were expecting it to be about a six month wait time. I was too numb to cry. I felt a mixture of peace and acceptance, and maybe a bit of shock too. There was literally nothing I could do but wait.

There is so much more to my story that I could share, and I question what is most important to include here for you. But one thing stands out: nobody could look at my life and not believe in God. I'm not trying to convince you, but I hope you can see the miracles and freedom that come from keeping an open heart with God and having faith. Faith requires trust beyond our human comprehension, but when we develop that trust and relationship with God, all the bad and evil we face in this world and in our lives can be turned to good. I am a living testament to this.

During the wait for my surgery, I had a near-death experience that ultimately led to me being pushed to the top of the list when the hospital reopened, which thankfully ended up being much sooner than I had expected. In May, just two months after my first call, I received another one: they could book me for surgery in two weeks. I just needed to confirm that I could get flights, and they would provide all the necessary medical paperwork to get me into the country.

With God's grace, I found flights, located a third person willing to travel internationally during Covid, and booked our flights and apartment. The God moments would continue to unfold throughout the journey. From the third person who dropped everything last minute to be with me in a small corner apartment post-surgery to the surgeon's assistant being from the same town I was from, fluent in English, and a great comfort. And then there was the fact that I had to be in Barcelona for six weeks, just as the city opened for about eight weeks that summer. It closed again about a week after I returned home.

My healing journey was years in the making and included other medical interventions. I also discovered I'd had chronic Lyme disease for twenty years, so I had to tackle that. God was in the details, and I write to you today fully healed. And even better, I'm not only healed but *LIVING* again. FREE again. I lived in that hard neck brace for four and half years. But as soon as I got up from surgery, I was able to walk without my crutches; I was able to feel the flooring beneath my feet; I felt the temperature of my husband's breath as he leaned in to kiss my forehead. All miracles I don't take for granted.

Today, I can run again. I swim with my kids, I walk with my kids daily. I can take care of our household needs, drive around, shop for, and educate my children. I live a life I was told not to even hope for again. To settle for surviving and be happy to still be alive. But God called me for more, and He calls you for more too. We don't have to be prisoners to our circumstances. He didn't put us here to survive. We are here to live, and live fully! I believe healing is your birthright and that the blueprint for healing mentally and physically is in your body, though our mind often gets in the way.

One thing I can't leave without noting is how interesting it is to experience a mental illness crisis and a physical illness crisis back-to-back. When we reached out for help and support for my mental illness, we were very selective in who we told and who helped us. Not just from fear of judgement, but because it was so hard to speak of. The stigma is real. People who did find out about my mental illness would say things that they thought were helpful but weren't. One person said to me something that I will never forget. To this day I use this comment to remind me that we never know what someone else is going through. She said that upon seeing me at church, week after week with four kids in tow five years of age and under, "I thought you had it all together. You always seemed like you had it put together. Prepared, calm with the boys and a smile on your face. I had no idea you were hurting so badly inside." So much truth to her comment. I have lost friends to suicide and have even been caught off guard at some of the losses. Had I gone through with it, people would have been shocked that I was in so much pain.

Then I went through a very visible illness, one where I couldn't walk without support. If I didn't have my hard neck brace on, I couldn't even get out of bed; I would pass out on the floor. The physical pain of the migraines I experienced was impossible to hide.

People saw it, and when they asked how they could help our family, I didn't hesitate to tell them.

The stark difference in the way I was treated through these two experiences was interesting. I felt like mental illness was viewed as something contagious, as if people could "catch" it by coming too close to me, while my physical illness was met with much more compassion. I'm not sure if it's because mental illness feels scarier or less tangible to people—since you can't see it—or if it's simply that they don't know how to help. For centuries, culture has painted mental illness through extreme examples—people in straitjackets, people society has labeled as "crazy" in psychiatric facilities, or through violence in the news—so it's no wonder many still carry subconscious fear or misunderstanding. In reality, most mental illness is quiet, hidden, and lived out in silence, not spectacle. Hopefully this is changing with the rise in mental health awareness since Covid and the increase in suicides.

I just challenge you: don't be afraid to ask the hard questions. *"Are you thinking of hurting yourself? Are you suicidal now, or have you been in the past? Are you happy? What brings you joy?"*

See people, really see them. A life is always worth the effort, time, money or anything else necessary to save it. That includes your own. If I could change anything about my story it would be how long I waited to share fully with my husband how bad I was suffering. Please be brave and open up to someone who you trust to help you get to the other side of whatever you are facing.

If you take anything away from my chapter, I hope it is this. That freedom from whatever prison you are facing is possible. Healing is possible. That God is as real as the breath you breathe and that joy, love, laughter are all things that you will feel again. Don't give up hope, IT IS WORTH FIGHTING FOR! *I promise.*"

When I interviewed Brooke on my podcast, *Soul Soldier Speaks*, she shared something deeply powerful that relates to what she just shared here with you all that needs a whole lot more attention and understanding. She said she would take the physical illness and all the pain that came with it over the mental illness any day. For her, being a prisoner in her own mind felt infinitely more lonely and terrifying than being a prisoner in her body. With her physical illness, at least she had support. People came alongside her, walking with her through the agony. She wasn't fighting alone.

This is a crucial point we need to address when it comes to mental illness. The isolation, the silence, the belief that you have to endure it by yourself; this is where so much of the destruction happens. We must change this narrative. People battling mental illness need to know they don't have to fight in the darkness alone. Reaching out, sharing the burden, and knowing you're not walking through it in isolation can make all the difference. We cannot afford to let anyone feel like they're battling by themselves, because that kind of solitude can lead to unimaginable pain and despair. It's time to offer the same compassion and support for mental illness that we give to physical illness. No one should be afraid to reach out for help, and no one should have to carry it alone.

Brooke's story is one of miracles, both seen and unseen. It's a powerful reminder that, no matter how deep the darkness, there is always hope for healing and freedom from our bondage. Brooke's faith in God, her perseverance, and her willingness to share her story have allowed her to rise from the ashes of despair, living a life she once thought impossible. Her story is a testament to the truth that freedom—both mental and physical—is always possible when we put our faith in God. And if you're walking through your own battle, just know: God's work in your life is far from over. I encourage you with deep love and belief in you to keep going. Your story is still being written.

CHAPTER 16

The Key to the Lock

We've explored the disconnection that broke us, the prisons that keep us bound, the heart of the matter, where freedom truly comes from, and the testimonies of those who have found release. Now, as we come to the end of these pages, it's important to name the key that unlocks every prison door. You've heard it woven through these stories, whispered in the testimonies, echoed in my own journey. So what is the key? What frees us from every chain, every circumstance that holds us captive?

SURRENDER AND OBEDIENCE . . .

Not the kind of surrender that signals defeat, but the kind that invites God, the only One who sees what we cannot, to work in and through our lives. So much of what we face in life is bigger than we are. Surrender and obedience begins with acknowledging this truth: this is bigger than me, so I must turn to the One bigger than me to guide me.

Jason Smith shared that, when he tried to be the "leader of his life," it never went well. I imagine a train flying off the tracks, barreling downhill with no way to stop. That's what life looks like when we insist on steering it ourselves: out of control, headed toward destruction. And even if it doesn't reach that level of intensity, I can assure you your life will always be more enriched when you let the Spirit lead. When Jason Smith finally surrendered and allowed God to take the lead, everything changed. A freedom entered his life that shattered the chains of everything that once held him captive.

Isn't this the truth for so many of us? How often do we try to lead our own lives, only to find ourselves stuck—burdened by pain, weighed down by choices, exhausted by the climb, and still no closer to freedom? I know I certainly can relate. Every time I've tried to control my own path, it only left me more lost, more broken, and more desperate for something bigger than me. That's because we are operating from the soul and EGO (Edging God Out).

But here's the shift: when I finally began to soften, when I loosened my grip and let God lead, when I stepped into deeper surrender, everything shifted. The chains that once kept me bound broke. The heaviness began to lift. And suddenly, the path forward became clear; not because I was in control, but because He was. And I assume you understand this: surrender doesn't erase the pain or make all of life's problems disappear. What it does is make the struggle bearable. It allows us to be led when we don't know what to do or where to go. It gives us a strength we don't have on our own and a peace we could never manufacture by ourselves.

THE POWER OF SURRENDER

When I think about surrender in my own life, my mind goes back to the summer of 2020, when our son Alex's struggles had reached a devastating breaking point. One day, the weight of it all had been crushing me so deeply, it all came to a head and I felt physically ill from the anguish. As I sat there in despair, I realized I couldn't carry this. It was far too heavy. It was beyond my ability to fix. In my desperation, I cried out to a God I had barely spoken to in a long time: *God, what do I do?*

And I heard: *Turn inward and surrender.*

It was a moment of piercing clarity, like lightning striking my heart. I realized the only thing I truly had control over was myself, not Alex's choices, not the outcome of his battle, only my actions and my responses. As parents, we carry the illusion that we can control our children's paths. But the truth is, we can only influence; they become their own people, responsible for their own decisions.

So when I surrendered, I wasn't giving up. I was handing over what was never mine to carry. I entrusted Alex to the God who sees what I cannot, and in return, God steadied my heart. He helped me focus on what I could control. Surrendering was both the hardest and most liberating decision of my life. I chose to not let Alex's choices and pain destroy my peace. From that moment on, an unshakable calm settled within me, a peace that held me even as we faced unimaginable heartbreak. That surrender didn't erase the external challenges, but it transformed me internally. It prepared me for the tragedy that would follow and gave me the strength to endure it.

A STEP OF OBEDIENCE: BAPTISM

And as if God wanted to anchor this lesson even deeper, He led me into another step of surrender and obedience during the very season I was writing this book.

Before we get into where he led me, let's talk about obedience for a moment. As I write these words and sit in the middle of financial ruin, God brought me to the book of Job. I can't help but relate to Job in so many ways, and I think many of us can. My husband and I have already endured the greatest loss imaginable, the loss of a child. And in the ashes of that grief, God revealed something to me: the two most important treasures in my life are Him and my family.

Everything outside of that is external. It's temporary. It doesn't matter in the light of eternity. It's wild how much meaning we attach to the things we own—our home, furniture, cars, objects that are here today and gone tomorrow. Yet, in that tension, God keeps pulling me back to Job and to His Word. He reminds me that when I turn to Him for direction and walk in obedience—even when it hurts, even when I don't understand—I will be led exactly where I am meant to go, and his direction always leads us to greater heights than we ever thought possible.

Through this, I am learning that abundance and breakthrough are not found in holding on, but in letting go. They are found on the other side of obedience when I become fully content and grateful; not because of anything external, but simply because of God's presence and my family's love. When I can rest in being content with God alone, I discover a wealth that can never be taken from me. And each day that I wake up with my family by my side, my gratitude overflows.

This truth echoed even louder as I studied Job 36:8–12:

"If people are bound in chains,

held fast by cords of affliction,

He tells them what they have done—

that they have sinned arrogantly.

He makes them listen to correction and

commands them to repent of their evil.

If they obey and serve Him, they will spend

the rest of their days in prosperity

and their years in contentment.

But if they do not listen, they will perish by the sword

and die without knowledge."

Affliction, then, is not always punishment; it is often correction. God uses suffering to expose what binds us and to call us back to Him. Obedience opens the door to blessing, while refusal leads only to destruction. This is why surrender and obedience go hand in hand.

They are the keys that unlock our prison doors and lead us into true freedom.

Now, back to where God led me in the process of writing this book: Baptism. I had been baptized as a baby, but I had never made that choice for myself. Over the past four years, since stepping back into church, I've watched God use me to lead so many friends and family into a relationship with Jesus. I've baptized my daughter, our foster child and her whole family, my assistant at work and her son, and I've witnessed the profound ripple effects of God's work through it all. One invitation opened the door to countless lives being changed. Had my trainer not invited me to church, I may never have rediscovered Jesus, and all of those who came after me might not have found Him either. That's the beauty of surrender and obedience: when you let God move into your life, He creates ripples far beyond what you could imagine.

But I hadn't yet stepped into the waters myself. Then one Saturday, while driving down the road listening to worship music, I suddenly heard a voice so clear: *It's time to get baptized.* It felt so random, so unexpected. I thought, *Okay, God . . . maybe I'll look at when the next baptism is later.* My walk with Jesus has been slow, yet steady. I still carry questions and doubts, wrestling with some of the core teachings of Christianity. And since, deep down, I believe that God and Jesus are far bigger than any one religion, baptism hadn't felt right for me—at least not yet.

Later that day, after recording a podcast, I felt a strong nudge to go to church. I hadn't been all summer; we'd been traveling and I had just been watching the sermons online. When I told my husband, who struggles with his own faith, that I wanted to go, he surprised me when he didn't hesitate to come. Within minutes, he and the kids were in the car with me. That in itself felt like God's hand at work. When we arrived, I walked in and saw it was baptism weekend. I had no idea. Surprised, I whispered in my heart, *Okay, God, I see You.*

Of course, I had spent time getting ready and curling my hair for the podcast earlier, had no change of clothes, and felt completely unprepared. But in that moment, I laughed inside at my superficial thought process as God reminded me "none of that matters."

As if that weren't enough, the pastor and his wife, who have been a meaningful part of my faith journey, were back from sabbatical that very day. Pastor Chad was preaching the final message in the Battle Ready series, and as he spoke the final words of a series that had been deeply resonating with me throughout, I felt God lining everything up, speaking straight to my heart: *It's time.*

I couldn't deny the strong pull, so despite still having doubts and questions, I said *yes.*

I stepped forward, completely unplanned, and was baptized. The pastor and his wife stood on one side of me with my husband on the other. My kids were there and some friends from my early faith journey just happened to be present too. It was as if God had orchestrated every detail. That moment was indescribably beautiful—the long-awaited next step in my walk with Jesus.

And here's what I can tell you with certainty: the deeper you go into surrender and obedience, the more peace and freedom you will experience. Through surrender, God becomes the Leader. And who better to lead than the One who sees what we cannot? From His higher vantage point, He guides us with clarity, purpose, and love. In His leading, we discover a peace this world cannot offer, because He sees the purpose beyond our pain and the meaning hidden in our prisons. And if we let Him, He will turn it all for good.

This is the paradox of freedom: it doesn't come by fighting harder, but by laying it down. It doesn't come by clinging tighter, but by opening our hands. And when you finally surrender, you will discover what I did, that even in your darkest valley, God has been writing a plot twist all along. **And in that plot twist is the freedom you never saw coming.**

It is God's desire that we bear much fruit. Everything we walk through becomes part of that process, bringing us into deeper alignment with Him, into alignment with truth, and into the kind of life that produces fruit that lasts.

And if you're wondering what I mean by "fruit," here is the fruit God calls us to bear:

- **Love**: selfless, unconditional care for others.

- **Joy**: a deep, steady gladness that isn't dependent on circumstances.

- **Peace**: inner calm and wholeness, even in life's storms.

- **Patience**: endurance and grace when times are hard or people are difficult.

- **Kindness**: compassion that seeks to bless others.

- **Goodness**: integrity, doing what is right in God's eyes.

- **Faithfulness**: loyalty and trustworthiness toward God and others.

- **Gentleness**: humility, strength under control.

- **Self-control**: mastery over impulses, thoughts, and actions.

It is this fruit, this evidence of God's Spirit within us, that brings fulfillment and shows us what true freedom looks like.

Every plot twist, every breakthrough in my life, and in the stories I've shared, has come in one way or another through surrender and an opening of the heart. Not striving. Not escaping. But releasing. Letting go. Falling into the arms of the only One strong enough to carry it all.

It doesn't crash in like lightning. It rises slowly, steadily—in the daily choice to let go. In the breath that whispers, *"I don't know how this ends, but I trust the One who does."* In the unclenching of your fists and the opening of your heart. In the quiet shift when fear stops being the loudest voice in the room.

Freedom is not a destination, it is a posture you return to, moment by moment. You don't have to wait for the relationship to heal, the bank account to recover, or the pain to disappear. You don't have to wait for the door to swing open. You can live free right here, right now, in the middle of the mess. That's the miracle—freedom is a covenant, not a condition.

I've sat with the incarcerated, the addicted, and the broken in some of the hardest places. People often ask how I can do it without fear. The answer is simple: I don't see labels. I see souls. And when you let God lead and you approach people soul-to-soul, something sacred opens. Respect forms. Trust follows. Walls fall. Hearts soften.

Like the man in the sauna who questioned whether gang members or inmates could ever change, I understood his doubts. He had seen destruction, violence, cycles of chaos. That's the enemy's work, and we've exposed it throughout these pages. But the truth is, many of them haven't yet encountered Jesus. And if they have, they haven't yet surrendered to Him. Because when they do, life begins to change in ways nothing else can explain.

I've seen it. I've watched men like Jason Smith and Jason Rudeen walk out of decades of destruction into the arms of Jesus. I've seen God redeem what the world had written off. I've witnessed what happens when someone dares to surrender and let God lead.

So now I offer this to you:

- You are not too far gone.

- Your pain is not shameful.

- Your mess is not unlovable.

- Your prison is not permanent.

You are intimately known by the One who can, the One who breaks chains, restores hope, and unlocks every door. Read that again. But you must choose Him. You must trust Him. You must return, again and again, to the place where freedom begins: surrender and obedience.

So what now? Now you commit. You say yes. Every day, we're invited to lay down what we can't carry and open our hands to the One who can. So I invite you: each morning, sit with God in prayer. Open your palms as a physical act of release and whisper, "God, I turn this over to You: this fear, this burden, this thing I can't fix. Show me the way. Show me what to do. Reveal what I need to see." Do this again and again. The more you practice, the more you'll discover that surrender and obedience isn't weakness, it's the very place where peace, freedom, and strength rise.

This book was written at the frequency of freedom. While you've held it in your hands, my prayer is that it's also been planted in your soul. Let it settle. Let it guide you. Let it reach into the locked places within and set you free.

You have the key. You always did. Now go and live like it.

A prayer for you:

If you have not already done so and you are ready to invite Jesus into your life, here is a simple prayer you can say right now in your heart, mind, or out loud:

Jesus, I'm tired of doing this alone.

I believe You are who You say You are.

I believe You love me, and that You gave

Your life so I can truly live.

Today, I'm saying yes to You.

Yes to Your Grace..

Yes to Your freedom.

Yes to letting You lead.

I invite you into my life and open my heart to

allow you to make me new.

I give You my heart, my trust, and my yes from this day forward.

Amen.

CHAPTER 17

The Freedom Climb

Life is full of steep climbs. You know them—those seasons where every step feels heavier than the last, you're treading water, and quitting whispers louder than hope. We've all been there. Maybe your climb looks like grief that won't let go, a dream that feels just out of reach, or a battle that's left you more bruised than you care to admit. These uphill battles test more than our endurance; they test our faith. They ask for more than just our effort; they call for our surrender.

The climb is hard. But the climb is also holy. It strips away what's shallow, revealing what's real. And whether you're in the middle of it or on the other side, there's a deep renewal that happens when you invite God into your mess—when you allow Him to be your guide when you can't see and your strength when you have none. The closer you get to Him, the more aligned you become with truth and with the reality of who you are.

I wrote this chapter on the final morning of our island trip, the place this book was born. I had my journal and a heart full of expectation, hoping to witness a breathtaking sunrise that would mark this closing chapter. I could almost picture it: the sky igniting with color, the waves catching the light, God speaking through a radiant display of glory. But instead, the wind howled around me, the clouds swallowed the horizon, and for forty minutes I sat there shivering, waiting for the light.

It didn't come the way I had hoped. There was no grand burst of color, no dramatic unveiling—only a slow, hidden rise behind a thick wall of gray. And that's when I couldn't help but notice the contrast. Months earlier, I had written the final chapter of my first book, *The Rise of a Soul Soldier*, right here on this same island, in this same place, also with the sunrise as my backdrop. That morning was completely different. The sky was alive with color, the warmth of the sun pierced boldly through the clouds, and the ocean shimmered. God's voice spoke loud and clear through that sunrise, and it felt like the perfect ending for that book—a story about rising, hope, and beauty breaking through after the storm.

But this morning was different. It was gray, hidden, cold, and quiet. And as I sat there, God revealed to me that it was also perfect. Because the story of this book isn't about light bursting forth in brilliance all at once. It's about waiting in the shadows, trusting in the silence, learning that God is at work even when you can't see Him. It's about the kind of release that unfolds one surrendered and obedient step at a time.

I needed that sunrise. I needed to feel the discomfort, to sit in the waiting, to recognize that even when the light is obscured, God is still rising in the background. His presence isn't always loud, but it is always steady. His promises aren't always revealed in a blaze of glory, but they are always certain.

After shivering in the wind, I finally stepped inside just long enough to catch my breath. When I came back out, there it was—not blazing, but steady. Not loud, but sure. The sun had been climbing all along, even when I couldn't see it. At that moment, God put this message on my heart: this is the climb toward freedom. It rarely looks the way we imagine. It's slow. It's messy. It's uncomfortable. But all the while, God is moving. His light is rising in your life even when you can't see it or feel it. And just like that morning, there will be times when you step back into the cold and realize you were never waiting alone. The warmth was always on its way.

I almost gave up that morning. I almost walked away. But instead, I stepped inside for a moment, took a breath, and then stepped back out. That's when I realized how often we do the same thing with God. When life doesn't unfold the way we hoped, it's easy to shut our hearts to Him. It's easy to blame Him for the mess. I get it; I've felt that too. So if that's where you are, I see you and I honor you in that space. It is okay to be angry with God.

He invites us to lament. Lament simply means bringing your grief, confusion, disappointment, and unanswered questions to Him instead of carrying them alone. It's choosing honesty over hiding. Connection over withdrawal. Lament isn't a lack of faith—it's an expression of it. It says, God, this hurts, and I don't understand. God doesn't ask us to be strong in His presence. He asks us to be real.

And, here's what I learned that day: if you stick through the climb, through the difficulty, and keep the door of your heart open, even just a crack, everything changes. Give yourself permission to rest when you need to, but don't give up altogether. Because in time, you'll begin to see what's been there all along—God at work.

What He longs to do most is perform heart surgery: to take the places hardened by pain, shame, or fear, and soften them with His love. To turn our hearts back toward what is good and true. To remind us that in Him we are whole, we are enough, we are worthy.

God revealed to me that the climb is not a test of how much you can endure, it's an invitation to discover who you are with Him by your side. It's not about racing to the top, it's about letting the journey change you. It's about allowing God to meet you on the side of the mountain, in the wind, in the waiting, in the mess, and do what only He can do: transform you from the inside out.

There will be days you're sure you can't take another step. There will be seasons where the fog is so thick you can't see the summit. But the same God who met Paul in a prison cell, Job in the ashes when he had lost everything, and who has met me over and over in the middle of my pain, is the One who will carry you too. The climb will not crush you; it will shape you. It will reveal the resilience He's already placed inside you and the peace that's been waiting beneath the struggle.

And when the sun finally breaks through the clouds, you'll understand you didn't just survive the climb—you were transformed by it. You learned to trust when you couldn't see, to rest when you had no strength, and to keep moving even when the outcome was uncertain. That is where the plot twists happen. That is where divine redemption shows up in the most unexpected ways. Life rarely unfolds the way we expect. It's in the twists and turns, the unplanned detours, that transformation takes root.

I never imagined myself writing a book like this, with Jesus so present in my story and healing. Yet here I am: changed, renewed, transformed. What I've come to realize is that life is so much bigger than me. I am simply the vessel; He is the guide. It brings to mind the truth reflected in 1 Corinthians 1:27: "God doesn't call the qualified; He qualifies the called." When you open your heart to Him, you never know the extraordinary things He will do in and through you.

This book, these very words on the page, are the greatest plot twist of my life. I am deeply grateful that I kept my heart open and allowed God to work in and through me over these past four years. Without Him, I would not be standing here today, experiencing the steadiness and peace I now carry—peace that holds firm no matter the circumstance, the pain, or the hardship I face. And now, it is my deepest honor to speak that same truth and life into you—the one holding this book in your hands.

Everything you've read in these pages, every testimony, every truth, every glimpse of redemption points to this: you are not stuck where you are. Even if it feels hidden, even if it feels impossible, you are already standing in the middle of your own plot twist. Watch for the signs. Lean into the lessons. And above all, keep your heart open to God.

Don't give up when the night feels long or the climb feels unbearable. Restoration is not just for someone else's story, it's for yours too. One day, you'll look back and see that this season—this very climb—was part of your own beautiful plot twist, leading you where you were always meant to go; back into His arms.

And before I close, I want you to know this: you're right where you are supposed to be, even if you're still in process. You may carry doubts. You may wrestle with questions. You may not have all the same language or beliefs. That doesn't disqualify you—it simply makes you human. If Jesus feels close, lean in. If He feels distant, be honest. If faith feels fragile, let it be fragile. Freedom does not require certainty. It requires openness. The same Jesus who transformed my life has a way of meeting us right where we are, doubts and all. His love isn't fragile, and it isn't reserved for those who "get it right." His grace is bigger than our boxes, His mercy deeper than our understanding.

The plot twist isn't that life suddenly gets easy. The plot twist is that even here—even now—you are still loved, still held, and still becoming free.

So wherever you find yourself—on the mountain, in the valley, or somewhere in between—I pray you find the courage to keep climbing, the faith to keep trusting, and the grace to discover the plot twist God has already written for your life. Keep your heart open, because your story is still being written by the One who turns prisons into places of purpose and battles into victories. **This is the freedom you never saw coming.**

Closing Prayer

Jesus,

Thank You for being the steady light when the climb feels long and the wind cuts deep.

Thank You for rising even when we cannot see You.

Teach us to trust the process, to lean into Your strength, and to rest in Your presence when the way ahead feels uncertain.

Meet us in the middle of our climb and remind us that we are never alone on the mountain.

Shape us, change us, and lead us to the summit You have prepared for us.

And when we get there, may we look back with awe, not at how strong we were, but at how faithful You've been.

Amen.

The Freedom Toolbox

The freedom toolbox is a bonus reference section here for you when the prisons of life feel heavy and you need hope. Each chapter is organized around the common prisons we face, whether in our mind and heart, finances, relationships, behaviors, circumstances, or spirit.

Every entry gives you:

- The Scripture itself.

- The context to help you understand why it was written.

- A Plot Twist Connection that ties it to the theme of breaking free.

- A Life Application to put the truth into practice today.

- A Freedom Prayer you can make your own.

- A Journaling Prompt for reflection and devotion.

Treat it as a toolbox:

- When shame rises, flip to **Mind & Heart Prisons.**

- When financial stress feels overwhelming, open **Financial Prisons.**

- When rejection or broken relationships weigh heavy, read **Relational Prisons.**

- When addiction, control, or numbing drags you down, find strength in **Behavioral Prisons.**

- When illness, abuse, homelessness, or loss surrounds you, open **Situational Prisons.**

- When you feel far from God, turn to **Spiritual Prisons.**

You'll also find:

- Paul's "Freedom in Chains" story: proof that even in prison, you can be free.

- A Quick Reference section for the everyday battles that sneak up on us.

This toolbox is not exclusive and is not meant to replace your Bible, it's meant to be a bridge to it. Let it lead you back into God's Word, and most importantly, into His presence. Because no matter the prison, freedom is always possible when you walk with the One who can set you free.

MIND & HEART PRISONS

(self-hatred, shame, fear, perfectionism, hopelessness, trials)

MATTHEW 11:28–30

"Come to me, all you who are weary and burdened, and I will give you rest…"

Context: Jesus was speaking to people crushed under religious laws and life's burdens. His invitation is not to try harder, but to lay down the weight at His feet.

Plot Twist Connection: The greatest twists in life happen not through striving, but surrender. The chains of perfectionism, striving, and hopelessness break when we stop fighting alone and let God carry what we cannot.

Life Application: Freedom starts when you come to Jesus as you are. Lay your burdens down—your striving, shame, fear—and let Him lead.

Freedom Prayer:

"Jesus, I surrender my burdens and my battles. Teach me to walk in Your rest, not in my own strength. Set my soul free as I trust You."

Journaling Prompt:

- What burdens am I still carrying on my own?
- How would my life change if I truly laid them down?

ROMANS 8:1–2

"Therefore, there is now no condemnation for those who are in Christ Jesus…"

Context: Paul reminds us that in Christ, the penalty of sin and shame is broken.

Plot Twist Connection: Shame is one of the deepest prisons. But in Christ, shame's voice loses power; you are no longer defined by your failures.

Life Application: When shame whispers "you're unworthy," answer with truth: I am free in Christ.

Freedom Prayer:

"Lord, break the chains of shame and guilt. Help me walk in the truth that I am forgiven, loved, and made new."

Journaling Prompt:

- What shame-filled lies do I still listen to?
- What truth can I declare over them today?

JAMES 1:2–4

"Consider it pure joy, my brothers and sisters, whenever you face trials… because you know that the testing of your faith produces perseverance."

Context: James writes to believers under hardship, showing trials are not punishment but refinement.

Plot Twist Connection: The prisons of hardship are the very places God builds unshakable strength.

Life Application: Don't despise trials; let them shape you. On the other side of testing is maturity and freedom.

Freedom Prayer:

"God, give me strength in trials. Help me see beyond the pain to the growth You are producing in me."

Journaling Prompt:

- What trial am I currently facing that God might be using to grow me?
- Where have I seen perseverance grow in past struggles?

2 CORINTHIANS 5:17

"If anyone is in Christ, the new creation has come: The old has gone, the new is here!"

Context: Paul reminds followers that salvation doesn't just forgive, it transforms. The past no longer defines them.

Plot Twist Connection: Shame or self-hatred says you'll always be who you were. Jesus says you are new. That's freedom.

Freedom Prayer:

"Jesus, silence shame's voice. Help me live as the new creation I am with You."

Journaling Prompt:

- What "old" part of my story do I still let define me?
- How can I step into my "new" identity today?

PHILIPPIANS 4:6

"Do not be anxious about anything, but in every situation, by prayer and petition, with thanksgiving, present your requests to God."

Context: Written from prison, Paul teaches replacing worry with prayer.

Plot Twist Connection: Anxiety is a mental prison. The key is prayer—handing it over and receiving God's peace.

Life Application: Every anxious thought is an invitation to pray. Trade worry for gratitude and trust.

Freedom Prayer:

"Lord, I lay my anxieties before You. Fill my heart with peace that goes beyond understanding."

Journaling Prompt:

- What anxious thought do I need to hand over right now?
- Where could I practice gratitude instead of worry?

2 TIMOTHY 1:7

"For the Spirit God gave us does not make us timid, but gives us power, love and self-discipline."

Context: Paul encourages Timothy to be bold in faith, empowered by the Spirit.

Plot Twist Connection: Fear is a liar and a captor. God's Spirit equips us with the power of love, courage, and a sound mind to walk in freedom.

Life Application: When fear speaks, answer with God's truth: I have His Spirit, the power, love, and self-control.

Freedom Prayer:

"Holy Spirit, replace my fear with Your power, love, and strength."

Journaling Prompt:

- Where is fear keeping me small?
- How might I walk in power, love, and self-discipline today?

EPHESIANS 3:18–19

"…that you may have power… to grasp how wide and long and high and deep is the love of Christ…"

Context: Paul prays followers would experience Christ's love.

Plot Twist Connection: The prison of feeling unloved shatters under His immeasurable love.

Life Application: Ask God to help you feel His love daily, not just know it.

Freedom Prayer:

"Jesus, help me grasp Your love. Fill me with Your fullness."

Journaling Prompt:

- Do I live as if I am truly loved?
- How could I root myself deeper in His love today?

PSALM 139:13–14

"You created my inmost being; You knit me together in my mother's womb…"

Context: David praises God's intentional design.

Plot Twist Connection: Self-hatred is a lie. You are fearfully and wonderfully made.

Life Application: Speak this truth over yourself when self-criticism rises.

Freedom Prayer:

"Lord, thank You for making me wonderfully. Silence self-hatred with Your truth."

Journaling Prompt:

- What harsh words do I use against myself that God would never say?
- How can I replace them with His truth?

LAMENTATIONS 3:22–23

"Because of the Lord's great love we are not consumed… His mercies are new every morning."

Context: Jeremiah laments devastation yet clings to God's mercy.

Plot Twist Connection: Perfectionism and hopelessness collapse under mercy that renews daily.

Life Application: Each morning remind yourself: His mercy begins fresh today.

Freedom Prayer:

"God, thank You for mercy new each day. Let this hope sustain me."

Journaling Prompt:

- Where do I feel consumed right now?
- How does God's daily mercy bring me hope?

1 JOHN 1:9

"If we confess our sins, He is faithful and just to forgive… and purify us…"

Context: John assures believers that confession leads to forgiveness and cleansing, because God is faithful.

Plot Twist Connection: Guilt keeps us chained to the past (which is what the enemy wants). But God wants us free. Confession breaks the chain and opens the door to freedom.

Life Application: Don't hide your guilt. Bring it to God. He doesn't shame you, He purifies you.

Freedom Prayer:

"Faithful God, I confess my sins to You. Wash me clean and help me live free."

Journaling Prompt:

- What guilt am I still carrying that God has already forgiven?
- How can I walk lighter in His freedom?

MATTHEW 6:12

"Forgive us our debts, as we also have forgiven our debtors."

Context: Forgiveness is central to kingdom living. In the Lord's Prayer, Jesus ties our forgiveness to how we forgive others.

Plot Twist Connection: Holding onto unforgiveness is a prison. Releasing others frees your own soul.

Life Application: Choose forgiveness daily, deliberate practice, not as a feeling but as obedience.

Freedom Prayer:

"Father, forgive me as I forgive others. Free me from bitterness and fill me with grace."

Journaling Prompt:

- Who do I still need to forgive?
- What would it look like to release that today?

1 PETER 5:7

"Cast all your anxiety on Him because He cares for you."

Context: Peter reminds believers to humble themselves and trust God's care in their struggles. Humility looks like handing burdens to the One who cares.

Plot Twist Connection: Anxiety tries to convince you that you're alone. God cares deeply and carries your burdens.

Life Application: Don't carry what you're not meant to. Hand every worry over to Him, again and again.

Freedom Prayer:

"Father, I release my worries to You. Remind me daily that You care and are holding me."

Journaling Prompt:

- What specific worries am I holding onto?
- How can I practice giving them to God today?

ROMANS 2:1, 3–4

"You, therefore, have no excuse, you who pass judgment on someone else…"

Context: Paul rebukes hypocrisy—judging others while overlooking our own sin—and reminds us that it is God's kindness, not wrath, that leads us to repentance.

Plot Twist Connection: Judgment enslaves us in pride. Kindness sets us free.

Life Application: Lead with grace instead of judgment.

Freedom Prayer:

"Merciful God, forgive me for the times I've judged others. Help me extend the same kindness that You have shown me."

Journaling Prompt

- When have I judged others while forgetting my own need for grace?
- How has God's kindness, not condemnation, transformed me?

ROMANS 2:29

"No, a person is a Jew who is one inwardly; and circumcision is circumcision of the heart, by the Spirit…"

Context: Paul redefines identity: true belonging is not about outward labels but about a transformed heart.

Plot Twist Connection: Religion without heart change is another kind of prison.

Life Application: Live for God's approval, not human applause.

Freedom Prayer:

"God, circumcise my heart. Strip away performance and pride so I can live for You."

Journaling Prompt

- Where do I seek human approval over God's?
- What layers of my heart is God asking me to soften?

MATTHEW 5:3–12

"Blessed are the poor in spirit, for theirs is the kingdom of heaven…"

Context: Jesus begins the Sermon on the Mount by redefining blessing—not as worldly success, but as dependence on God.

Plot Twist Connection: The world calls "blessed" those who look strong and successful. Jesus calls "blessed" those who know their need.

Life Application: Embrace weakness as the doorway to God's presence.

Freedom Prayer:

"God, meet me in my poverty of spirit. Fill me with Your kingdom blessing."

Journaling Prompt:

- Which Beatitude speaks most to me right now?
- Where do I need to see weakness as a blessing instead of a curse?

FINANCIAL PRISONS

(debt, poverty, worth tied to performance)

ISAIAH 43:19

"See, I am doing a new thing! … I am making a way in the wilderness and streams in the wasteland."

Context: God spoke this to Israel in exile, promising renewal in barren places.

Plot Twist Connection: Wilderness seasons feel hopeless, but God specializes in making rivers flow where everything feels dry. When finances feel dry, God can bring rivers through deserts.

Life Application: Trust that God is doing something new, even when you can't see it yet. The desert can become the very place you encounter His provision.

Freedom Prayer:

"God, open my eyes to see the new thing You're doing. Give me hope in the dry places and faith to believe streams are coming. Bring streams of provision into my wilderness."

Journaling Prompt:

- Where do I feel financial wilderness right now?
- How might God already be making a way in it?

PHILIPPIANS 4:19

"And my God will meet all your needs according to the riches of His glory in Christ Jesus."

Context: Paul thanks the Philippians for generosity and assures them of God's supply.

Plot Twist Connection: Scarcity says there's not enough. Christ says your needs will be met.

Life Application: Treat God as your Source, not your paycheck.

Freedom Prayer:

"Father, meet my needs and teach me contentment in You."

Journaling Prompt:

- Where am I tempted to see money as my security instead of God?
- How have I seen God provide for me in the past?

MATTHEW 6:31–33

"Do not worry… But seek first His kingdom and His righteousness, and all these things will be given to you as well."

Context: Jesus redirects worry toward Kingdom-first priorities.

Plot Twist Connection: Money fear is a prison; freedom comes in seeking Him first.

Life Application: Shift focus from anxiety about provision to pursuing His Kingdom.

Freedom Prayer:

"Lord, align my heart to seek You above everything else."

Journaling Prompt:

- Where am I seeking provision more than God's kingdom?
- What step could I take to seek Him first in my finances?

PROVERBS 22:7

"The rich rule over the poor, and the borrower is slave to the lender."

Context: Wisdom on the reality of debt's control.

Plot Twist Connection: Debt can shackle. Awareness is step one to freedom.

Life Application: Make a plan toward financial freedom—small faithful steps.

Freedom Prayer:

"God, help me break free from the bondage of debt and live wisely."

Journaling Prompt:

- What debt weighs most heavily on me?
- What practical first step can I take toward freedom?

JOB 1:21

"The Lord gave and the Lord has taken away; may the name of the Lord be praised."

Context: After devastating loss, Job worships rather than curses God.

Plot Twist Connection: True wealth isn't possessions—it's a surrendered heart.

Life Application: Anchor your worth in God, not your accounts.

Freedom Prayer:

"Lord, help me praise You in plenty and in loss."

Journaling Prompt:

- Do I measure wealth by money or by God's presence?
- How can I practice praising Him in all circumstances?

JOB 23:10

"But He knows the way that I take; when He has tested me, I will come forth as gold."

Context: Job understands trials as refining fire.

Plot Twist Connection: Financial hardship can refine us. It does not define or destroy us if we choose to see it this way and seek God in the middle of our mess.

Life Application: See scarcity and setbacks as refining in God's hands.

Freedom Prayer:

"God, refine me until I shine with Your glory."

Journaling Prompt:

- What financial struggle is refining me right now?
- How can I see it as part of God's process of making me gold?

ACTS 5:1–5

"Now a man named Ananias, together with his wife Sapphira, also sold a piece of property. With his wife's full knowledge he kept back part of the money for himself…"

Context: In the early church, Ananias and Sapphira lied about money, pretending to give more than they did. Their deceit cost them their lives.

Plot Twist Connection: Money reveals the heart. When we cling to appearances or dishonesty, finances become a prison. True freedom is integrity before God.

Life Application: Be honest with God and with yourself about money. He desires truth in the inward parts, not performance.

Freedom Prayer:

"God, free me from the temptation to find worth in wealth or appearances. Teach me integrity and trust in You as my provider."

Journaling Prompt:

- Where am I tempted to hide or pretend when it comes to money?
- What would financial integrity before God look like for me?

MARK 8:14–21

"Do you still not understand?"

Context: The disciples worried about bread when Jesus was warning them about spiritual blindness. They missed that the Bread of Life was with them.

Plot Twist Connection: Worrying about lack blinds us to the abundance already present. The real prison isn't financial shortage—it's lack of trust.

Life Application: Watch what "yeast" you let rise in your heart—fear, greed, control—or trust in God.

Freedom Prayer:

"Jesus, open my eyes to see Your provision already with me. Teach me to trust You instead of fearing lack."

Journaling Prompt:

- Where have I focused more on what I don't have than on Jesus' provision?
- What "yeast" (fear, greed, control) is spreading in my heart?

RELATIONAL PRISONS

(codependency, rejection wounds, toxic cycles)

EPHESIANS 5:21

"Submit to one another out of reverence for Christ."

Context: Paul teaches that mutual submission in marriage reflects Christ's love.

Plot Twist Connection: Control and selfishness are prisons in relationships. True freedom is found in love that yields and serves.

Life Application: Choose humility and mutual honor. Marriage flourishes when Christ is the center. Practice humility, listening, and service in all your closest relationships.

Freedom Prayer:

"Jesus, teach me humility in my marriage and help me honor, love, and serve as You do."

Journaling Prompt:

- Where do I resist humility in my closest relationships?
- How can I practice mutual submission and honor today?

PSALM 27:10

"Though my father and mother forsake me, the Lord will receive me."

Context: David declares God's unwavering acceptance.

Plot Twist Connection: Rejection wounds lose power when you rest in God's embrace.

Life Application: When rejected, rehearse God's reception of you.

Freedom Prayer:

"Father, heal my rejection wounds with Your embrace."

Journaling Prompt:

- Where do I still feel the sting of rejection?
- How does God's embrace answer that wound?

GALATIANS 1:10

"Am I now trying to win the approval of human beings, or of God? …"

Context: Paul refuses to live for human approval.

Plot Twist Connection: People-pleasing and codependency enslave; God's approval frees.

Life Application: Live for God's "Well done, my good and faithful servant," not public applause.

Freedom Prayer:

"God, free me from people-pleasing. Let me live for Your approval alone."

Journaling Prompt:

- Where am I seeking human approval more than God's?
- What would change if I lived for His "Well done"?

EPHESIANS 3:18–19

"…to grasp how wide and long and high and deep is the love of Christ…"

Context: Paul prays that we would experience, not just know, Christ's limitless love.

Plot Twist Connection: One of the cruelest prisons is believing you're unlovable. Christ's love is bigger than your doubts.

Life Application: Ask God to help you experience His love daily—not just as head knowledge, but heart reality.

Freedom Prayer:

"Jesus, help me grasp the depth of Your love. Fill me with the fullness of Your presence."

Journaling Prompt:

- Do I believe I am truly loved by God?
- How can I open myself to experience that love more deeply?

JOHN 10:27–29

"My sheep listen to my voice; I know them, and they follow me. I give them eternal life, and they shall never perish; no one will snatch them out of my hand."

Context: Jesus describes the intimacy between Himself and His followers—a relationship of recognition, security, and belonging.

Plot Twist Connection: Rejection and betrayal are painful prisons, but Jesus' voice calls us His own, and no one can take us from His hand.

Life Application: Anchor your identity in the One who knows your name and never rejects you.

Freedom Prayer:

"Jesus, let me hear Your voice above the noise of rejection. Remind me I am held securely in Your hand."

Journaling Prompt:

- Where am I still seeking belonging in human relationships?
- How does knowing I am secure in Jesus free me from that striving?

BEHAVIORAL PRISONS

(addictions, avoidance, control, numbing)

JOHN 8:36

"So if the Son sets you free, you will be free indeed."

Context: Jesus promises a freedom deeper than circumstance.

Plot Twist Connection: Addictions offer escape but enslave; Jesus truly frees.

Life Application: Seek Jesus as Deliverer, not another coping mechanism. Lasting freedom comes not from fixing yourself, but from knowing Jesus personally.

Freedom Prayer:

"Jesus, I say yes to You. Set me free in the places I am bound. Be the Lord of my life and the Savior of my soul."

Journaling Prompt:

- Where am I looking for escape instead of freedom?
- What would it look like to invite Jesus into that space?

ROMANS 12:2

"Do not conform... but be transformed by the renewing of your mind."

Context: Transformation comes by truth reshaping our thinking.

Plot Twist Connection: Numbing and control grow from toxic thought loops; truth rewires.

Life Application: Replace lies with Scripture daily; let God retrain your mind.

Freedom Prayer:

"God, renew my mind with Your truth."

Journaling Prompt:

- What thought patterns keep me stuck?
- What truth can I speak over them today?

EPHESIANS 6:11

"Put on the full armor of God, so that you can take your stand against the devil's schemes."

Context: Paul teaches believers that life is a spiritual battle requiring spiritual armor: truth, righteousness, faith, salvation, God's Word, and prayer.

Plot Twist Connection: Avoidance, compulsions and the prisons of fear, lies, and temptation are battles of the soul. Freedom comes when you learn to fight with truth instead of being crushed by lies.

Life Application: Daily choose to "put on" God's armor: remind yourself of truth, guard your heart, and wield Scripture when lies attack.

Freedom Prayer:

"God, clothe me in Your armor for today's battle. Strengthen me to stand firm in truth and walk in victory through Jesus."

Journaling Prompt:

- Which piece of God's armor do I most need to put on today?
- How can I actively use it against lies I'm battling?

1 CORINTHIANS 10:13

"No temptation has overtaken you except what is common to mankind… God is faithful; He will… provide a way out."

Context: Temptation is universal, but God always provides an exit.

Plot Twist Connection: The "trap" isn't final—God's escape route is real.

Life Application: When tempted, pause and ask, "Where's Your way out, Lord?" Then take it.

Freedom Prayer:

"God, help me see and take Your escape route."

Journaling Prompt:

- What temptations feel overwhelming to me?
- How has God already given me a way out before?

HEBREWS 12:1

"Let us throw off everything that hinders and the sin that so easily entangles..."

Context: The life of faith is a race; travel light.

Plot Twist Connection: Habits and coping mechanisms tangle; freedom means shedding weight.

Life Application: Name what entangles you—and throw it off with God's help.

Freedom Prayer:

"Lord, strip away what hinders me so I can run free."

Journaling Prompt:

- What habits or coping mechanisms are weighing me down?
- What's one step I can take to throw them off with God's help?

GALATIANS 2:20

"I have been crucified with Christ and I no longer live, but Christ lives in me. The life I now live in the body, I live by faith in the Son of God, who loved me and gave himself for me."

Context: Paul declares his old self has died, and his new life is lived in Christ's power.

Plot Twist Connection: Addiction, control, and self-effort lose their grip when you realize it's no longer you striving, but Christ living in you.

Life Application: Stop fighting in your own strength. Let the Spirit live through you.

Freedom Prayer:

"Jesus, I lay down my striving and self-effort. I invite You to lead me, so You may work in and through my life."

Journaling Prompt:

- Where am I still trying to fight battles in my own strength?
- What would it look like to let Christ live through me here?

SITUATIONAL PRISONS

(illness, abuse, homelessness, incarceration)

PSALM 34:18

"The Lord is close to the brokenhearted and saves those who are crushed in spirit."

Context: David wrote this psalm in a season of fear and anguish. God's nearness was his lifeline.

Plot Twist Connection: Suffering feels isolating, but God moves closer. Loss often feels like the deepest prison. Yet it's here God draws nearest—turning ashes into beauty, pain into purpose.

Life Application: Invite God into the raw spaces of your pain and/or grief. He is not distant; He is present with you in every tear.

Freedom Prayer:

"Lord, stay near me when my spirit feels crushed. Hold me in my brokenness. Heal the places I cannot fix. Turn my sorrow into something only You can redeem."

Journaling Prompt:

- Where do I feel most crushed in spirit?
- How can I invite God into that exact place?

LAMENTATIONS 3:22–23

"Because of the Lord's great love we are not consumed... His mercies are new every morning."

Context: Hope rises in the ruins through God's steady mercy.

Plot Twist Connection: Each dawn carries mercy enough for today's pain.

Life Application: Greet the morning naming mercies—out loud.

Freedom Prayer:

"God, sustain me today with new mercy."

Journaling Prompt:

- What mercy did God show me today, even in the middle of hardship?
- How can I hold onto that as hope?

2 CORINTHIANS 12:9

"My grace is sufficient for you, for My power is made perfect in weakness."

Context: Paul's "thorn" remained; God's power rested on him.

Plot Twist Connection: Weakness is not your prison—it's a platform for His strength.

Life Application: Stop despising your limitations; lean hard on His grace.

Freedom Prayer:

"Lord, let Your power shine in my weakness."

Journaling Prompt:

- What weakness frustrates me most right now?
- How could it be the very place God wants to show His power?

PSALM 46:1

"God is our refuge and strength, an ever-present help in trouble."

Context: A declaration of God's protection amid chaos.

Plot Twist Connection: Abuse, danger, and crisis don't erase His presence—He is your safe place.

Life Application: Run to God as refuge; set safe boundaries with wisdom.

Freedom Prayer:

"God, be my safe place when life feels unsafe."

Journaling Prompt:

- Where do I need to seek refuge in God right now?
- What boundaries might He be inviting me to set?

HEBREWS 7:25

"Therefore He is able to save completely those who come to God through Him, because He always lives to intercede for them."

Context: The writer of Hebrews reminds believers that Jesus is our eternal High Priest, always interceding on our behalf.

Plot Twist Connection: Illness, imprisonment, or loss can make us feel forgotten. But Jesus Himself is praying for you right now. You are never unseen.

Life Application: When life feels unbearable, picture Jesus interceding for you at the Father's side.

Freedom Prayer:

"Jesus, thank You for interceding for me. Remind me I am never alone or forgotten."

Journaling Prompt:

- Where do I feel forgotten in my suffering?
- How does it change things to know Jesus is interceding for me?

SPIRITUAL PRISONS

(feeling abandoned by God, religious hurt, disconnection from truth)

1 PETER 2:9

"But you are a chosen people, a royal priesthood… called you out of darkness into His wonderful light."

Context: Peter reminded persecuted believers of their true identity in Christ—chosen, royal, and belonging.

Plot Twist Connection: Religious pain can attack our identity; God names you chosen and called. One of the enemy's greatest lies is that you are worthless. God's truth says you are chosen and loved.

Life Application: Declare your identity in Christ where wounds accuse you. When you feel unseen or rejected, declare God's truth over yourself: I am chosen. I am His.

Freedom Prayer:

"God, silence every lie that says I'm not enough. Heal my wounds and remind me I am chosen, loved, and called into Your light."

Journaling Prompt:

- Where do I still believe lies about my worth?
- How can I declare God's truth over my identity today?

ROMANS 8:38–39

"Neither death nor life… nor anything else in all creation, will be able to separate us from the love of God…"

Context: Paul assures the church nothing can sever them from God's love.

Plot Twist Connection: One of the cruelest prisons is believing God has abandoned you; this promise smashes that lie.

Life Application: When loneliness whispers, declare: Nothing separates me from His love.

Freedom Prayer:

"Father, when I feel alone, remind me Your love never leaves me."

Journaling Prompt:

- Where do I feel most alone right now?
- How does this verse remind me that God's love is unbreakable?

JOHN 14:6

"I am the way and the truth and the life. No one comes to the Father except through Me."

Context: Jesus offers Himself—not a system—as the path to God.

Plot Twist Connection: Religion may wound; Jesus heals and restores.

Life Application: Follow Christ Himself—know His voice, walk in His truth.

Freedom Prayer:

"Jesus, heal the wounds from religion. Let me know You as the Way, the Truth, and the Life."

Journaling Prompt:

- Where has religion hurt me or left me disillusioned?
- How can I seek Jesus Himself beyond systems?

FREEDOM IN CHAINS: PAUL'S STORY

ACTS 16:25–26

"About midnight, Paul and Silas were praying and singing hymns to God, and the other prisoners were listening to them. Suddenly there was such a violent earthquake that the foundations of the prison were shaken. At once all the prison doors flew open, and everyone's chains came loose."

Context: Paul and Silas, imprisoned for their faith, chose worship instead of despair. God's power shook the prison walls and set every captive free. Paul wrote much of the New Testament from prison. Though his body was confined, his soul was free, and the gospel spread.

Plot Twist Connection: Worship in the darkest place can break chains—not just yours, but others'.

Life Application: Sing and pray even in your midnight hour. Your worship carries freedom.

Freedom Prayer:

"God, give me a song to sing in the midnight hour. Shake my chains loose as I choose to worship You."

Journaling Prompt:

- What is my "midnight hour" right now?
- How could worship shift my perspective in it?

PHILIPPIANS 1:12–14

"Now I want you to know, brothers and sisters, that what has happened to me has actually served to advance the gospel. As a result, it has become clear throughout the whole palace guard and to everyone else that I am in chains for Christ. And because of my chains, most of the brothers and sisters have become confident in the Lord and dare all the more to proclaim the gospel without fear."

Context: Paul's faithful words while imprisoned reminded the church that his chains were not wasted. They encouraged others to live boldly for Christ.

Plot Twist Connection: Paul's story proves that external prisons cannot cage an internally free soul. Even in chains, he became a voice of freedom.

Life Application: Look for how God is using your hard places to encourage others. Your circumstances don't define your freedom. Like Paul, you can worship, witness, and walk in peace—even when life feels like a prison.

Freedom Prayer:

"Lord, use my story, even the painful parts, to strengthen and inspire others. Teach me Paul's freedom. No matter my circumstances, let me live in Your truth, carry Your peace, and shine Your light."

Journaling Prompt:

- How might my current struggle serve to encourage someone else?
- Who could be impacted by my story of perseverance?

2 TIMOTHY 2:9

"…because I suffer for the gospel, even to the point of being chained like a criminal. But God's word is not chained."

Context: Paul reminds Timothy that though he himself was chained, the gospel was still free and unstoppable.

Plot Twist Connection: Circumstances can chain a person, but nothing can chain God's Word.

Life Application: Trust that God's Word is still alive and active even when you feel limited.

Freedom Prayer:

"God, let me live in confidence that Your Word cannot be chained. May it run free through my life so that no matter my circumstance, I feel the freedom still available to me even in the middle of my storm."

Journaling Prompt:

- Where do I feel limited right now?
- How does God's Word speak freedom beyond those limits?

CLOSING WORD

Freedom is not found in perfect circumstances, but in the presence of the One who meets us in every prison. Whether your chains are in your mind, your finances, your relationships, your habits, your situations, or even in your spirit; Jesus has already declared that the door is open.

The verses in this Freedom Toolbox are not magic words, they are living promises from the God who never fails. Let them be your lifeline in the midnight hour, your anchor in the storm, and your battle cry when lies and fear close in.

Remember: the prison is not the end of your story. God is the Author of every plot twist, and He has already written freedom, hope, and victory into yours.

Journaling Prompt:

- Which "prison" feels heaviest to me right now?
- Which verse from this appendix do I want to carry as my lifeline?
- How can I take one step forward today in faith, trusting God?

Step forward in faith, my freedom walkers, and keep declaring His truth over your life. And never forget, the Son sets us free, **making us free indeed.**